The Eternal Triangle

Susan Quilliam is a writer, psychologist and counsellor who has herself had experience of the Eternal Triangle.

Susan Quilliam

The Eternal
Triangle

Pan Original Pan Books
London, Sydney and Auckland

First published 1990 by
Pan Books Ltd
Cavaye Place, London SW10 9PG

9 8 7 6 5 4 3 2 1

Copyright © Transformation Management 1990

ISBN 0 330 31332 0

Photoset by Parker Typesetting Service, Leicester

Printed by Clays Ltd, St Ives plc

Contents

Acknowledgements

I wish to thank the many people and organisations who have helped me create this book.

My particular thanks to the people who talked to me so openly and bravely about their experience of the Eternal Triangle. Whether their interviews have been used in full, or whether they have been used in a more general sense to inform my writing, this book would not exist without them and their courage.

My thanks, too, to all the many people who networked for me to gather interviewees; in particular, gratitude to Eva Lewicki and *Time Out* for mentioning this book on their letter page.

Next, my thanks to all those who have allowed me to benefit from their professional expertise and experience, particularly: Caroline Bailey of the Brook Advisory Centre; Norman Blumenfeld of the Jewish Marriage Guidance Council; Jane Lloyd of the Westminster Pastoral Foundation; Mike Owen of Human Systems Consultancy; the Scottish Marriage Guidance Council; Zelda West-Meads of Relate; and, particularly, Judi Hildebrand of the Institute of Family Therapy for her enormous help in developing ideas and thinking it all through.

Also, my thanks to everyone on the production side, especially to Barbara Levy, my agent, for believing in the book in the first place, and to Judith Hannam and Hilary Davies of Pan Books for being brave enough to commission it!

Finally, to those around me who by their love and support have made this book possible: Caroline, Evelyn, Piers, Tony, Trevor, and, most especially, Ian.

Introduction

Is there anything so wonderfully exciting, yet so essentially terrifying as the Eternal Triangle? In a world where we all spend our time, consciously or unconsciously, looking for a love that is ours and ours alone, the idea of having affairs is both deeply disturbing and at the same time deliciously arousing. We love and hate them, deny them, judge them, condemn them – and seek them out time and time again.

If you are reading this book with no experience of the eternal triangle, then you are in a minority. Over sixty per cent of people in Britain today take a lover outside their primary relationship*. Most of us at some time are on one point or another of the triangle.

Why this fascination with three-way love? Perhaps it is the fact that we all want to be wanted, so having the possibility of two people loving us is inevitably more compelling than the thought of a single love. In an age where Having It All has become a way of life, why should we not find exciting the idea of having all the love we can get?

Perhaps, though, the fascination lies elsewhere – in doing something forbidden, taking a risk, stepping outside permitted boundaries. It may be the excitement of affairs which attracts us, as lover, as roaming partner – or as voyeur. For above and beyond even the sixty per cent of people who have affairs, are the millions more who buy novels about the eternal triangle, who go to see films about dangerous liaisons, who avidly read in the popular press about others who have broken the rules.

It may be a far more serious business, however. In these days of increasing divorce, a high proportion of relationships end

* *Adultery: A Study of Love and Betrayal* by Annette Lawson, Basil Blackwell, p75.

through one of the partners having an affair. If we reach a point in our partnership where the joy has diminished and a new love arrives before the old one has departed, then even if for only a short while, we will be part of a threesome. For many of us, the eternal triangle is a stepping-stone to real happiness.

And yet, and yet ... we live in a world where the eternal triangle is a threat on a number of levels. Firstly, it goes against all the myths of true love that have informed our adolescence, and that still, through films and literature, inform our adulthood. Real love is seen as monogamous, shared love as tarnished; if we truly loved our partner then we would not need anyone else.

Equally, the eternal triangle challenges the myth of the happy ending. If such things can happen, if the love we depend on can ever be threatened so deeply, then things may not be All Right In The End. The world may not be as secure a place as we have always wanted it to be, and we ourselves may not be the lovable people we thought we were.

In day-to-day terms, too, the eternal triangle is to be feared, for it destroys relationships. If our partner takes another lover, he or she will have less time for us, will prefer that lover to us, may eventually leave us to cope on our own with children, a mortgage and a job. If we are the lover concerned, then our future happiness may be threatened by someone else, who by hanging on to their spouse is going to deprive us of love for the rest of our lives. If we ourselves are taking a lover, then our life is turned into chaos as we strive to please everyone and still follow our hearts.

So we barricade ourselves against the threat of the eternal triangle with all the means at our disposal: religious laws, moral strictures, legal contracts and medical pronouncements of doom. We criticize colleagues who take lovers, we debar from our social circle those who have left their spouses, we write diatribes against adultery, mistresses and extra-marital sex.

And, in whatever position we find ourselves on the triangle, we suffer, lying awake at night because we want our threatened love to survive.

And yet, and yet ... it still happens. People still take lovers, still have affairs, still get drawn in, time and time again.

I first began to explore the issue of eternal triangles when I myself became involved in one. Stunned by the effect this had on my entire life, I began to explore three-way relationships. Talking to friends, reading the available psychological literature, drawing on my professional knowledge, I wanted to understand why eternal triangles happened, how they happened, how they kept on happening against all the odds.

I walked headlong into a barrage of mixed messages. The professional literature, the psychological textbooks, the statistical surveys told me about figures, facts, reasons and ratios. I was offered a picture of a 'type' of adulterer, a concept of a 'standard' eternal triangle, a set 'pattern' of affairs. Neatly tied up and packaged, and carefully analysed into 'causes and effects', these theories said quite clearly that if we controlled ourselves and our urges, if we ensured that our primary relationships were satisfactory, if we kept to the rules, if we were good, then the eternal triangle would never happen.

What I was hearing from those who had been in the triangle was a very different story. Here were no facts or questionnaires; here were raw emotions. Here were no types or patterns; each story was a unique account of pain and love, conflict and heartbreak. I met 'adulterers' who cried as they told me how they hadn't wanted to fall in love, but had. I met 'abandoned spouses' who knew beyond all shadow of doubt that their relationships had been good until 'the lover' came along. I met lovers who still lay awake at night, four years later, thinking about what could have been. When set alongside these very different experiences, all the rules, guidelines and categorizations seemed totally irrelevant. I began to realize that things were not as simple as I had first supposed.

It was obvious that a new model was needed, one that stepped outside simplistic, generalized explanations, the idea that affairs can be categorized, and the assumption that affairs don't happen to nice people. What was needed was a model that explained how affairs really happened. First, however, I needed more information, more people to talk to. I needed to find out, from the people who knew, what the experience of the eternal triangle is really like.

I therefore asked friends, and many trusted me enough to confide in me. I networked, through colleagues and acquaintances – even through someone I met on the London Underground! I contacted key professionals with specific expertise in the area of relationships. I enrolled the help of some listings magazines – and then spent several dozen hours on the phone as the calls came flooding in. I was invited to dinner by one 'pentangle'. I interviewed other people in the park, in their homes, in my home – even, on one occasion, on a traffic roundabout! Many interviewees took their courage in both hands and contacted, on my behalf, past partners and past lovers in order to get their side of the story. In the end I explored over fifty triangles, and heard second-hand about many more.

Slowly, but quite steadily, ideas began to emerge. I was certainly seeing a phenomenon which was, to my mind, not simplifiable into types or categories. There were patterns, but not those which could be categorized as the 'Casanova pattern' or the 'serious affair pattern'. Rather, I was seeing the patterns of relationship dynamics: that is, the process that goes on as interactions ebb and flow, the slow movements of triangles evolving from start to finish, the sudden changes as partnerships take on new configurations. These 'process patterns' were constant across all the triangles I explored, and they suggested to me that what was needed was not a series of generalizations or categories, but a flexible model that could be applied to any individual triangle and still be relevant.

The final piece of the jigsaw fell into place when I met one particular professional, Judi Hildebrand from the Institute of Family Therapy. In the course of two electric meetings, where we flung ideas, concepts, theories and evidence from one to the other, the whole model came together.

I had already known of and worked with the ideas of systemic family therapy. I had begun to grasp its principles: that any relationship is an evolving entity that can be understood in terms of emotional movements – loops and spirals, both stable and developing. Faced as I was with several hundred hours of tape-recordings of just such emotional movements, systemic thinking seemed to me to be the ideal framework into which to slot my discoveries and make sense of them.

I worked with systems ideas for a while, taking the basic concepts but applying them in a new way, adapting them to fit the eternal triangle, developing fresh approaches where the old ones didn't quite match. In the end, the model gave me all the elements I wanted. It got rid of the categorization and the generalization, it stepped totally outside the idea that only 'bad people' ever suffered from affairs; it offered an explanation that could be applied equally to any particular triangle and any individual situation. Best of all, it offered some practical suggestions as to what to do — to enter, maintain, end or destroy a triangle. With this new perspective, and the interviews I had done, I was ready to begin to write.

This book is not a theoretical one. Quite simply, the main body of it consists of the words of the interviewees themselves, all of whom have been in the eternal triangle, some of whom still are. These people, whose ages range from early twenties to sixties, have had the courage to open their lives, often risking their relationships and their credibility in order to do so. All the people I spoke to contributed to the ideas and structure of this book, even though in the end, faced with so much rich material, I had to choose the most representative interviews for transcribing in full, and leave others out.

My interviewees' stories are edited, but in every case the words are their own spoken or written accounts, and the edited versions have been approved by their originators. These stories have not been 'improved' or dramatized. This is what actually happened and this is how the people involved actually feel.

Alongside and interwoven with the stories is the conceptual framework which they together suggest. The first two chapters of the book introduce the basics of the new perspective, interleaving with interviewees' stories to give practical examples of what is happening. In the following five chapters certain elements crucial to eternal triangles are explored, though by this point, the stories themselves have taken over, each with its own brief commentary showing that it is possible to apply all the ideas to any individual situation. There follow five extended interviews, some presenting the same story from several different people's viewpoints. The closing chapter once more comes back to the concepts presented, in order to suggest practical action; the appendix lists resources for further reading or obtaining counselling.

The ideas that emerge in this book may be new, but they are not easy ones. I found much to challenge the common assumptions about eternal triangles, and much to oppose the usual viewpoints that society holds.

In common with many people, I used to believe that affairs began and ended unbidden, as lightning strikes. In fact, it quickly became clear that nothing is further from the truth. Acts of God can sometimes create relationships, but affairs are more normally dynamics – moving, evolving interactions with their own traceable development, maintenance and resolution. That was for me a comforting thought, for if we can really understand eternal triangles, really get to grips with what they are about, then we can begin to understand them, predict them, maybe even take charge of them.

Another commonly held belief is that those who have the affair – the 'erring' partner and his or her lover – are those who create it, that only two people are involved in what is happening. I discovered, however, that the emotional dynamics in a three- (or four-, or five-) sided relationship are so interdependent that everyone is involved; everyone helps to create the situation that eventually transpires.

Finally, our society works on the presupposition that affairs are always and in all circumstances a bad idea, that all relationships which include a third party are naturally flawed. However, I found a great deal of evidence to contradict this, from interviewees for whom an affair had created a totally positive change in their lives or their relationships.

In the sense that it will challenge you, therefore, this book is far from being an 'easy read'. It offers a new perspective on relationships in general and on eternal triangles in particular, a perspective which will almost certainly contradict some of your most basic assumptions about the way relationships work.

If you are in crisis, don't try to read this book yet. If your partner has just announced the start of an affair, if your lover has just announced an intention to leave, first take all the time you need to cry, shout, scream. Get all the support you deserve from friends and family. Cream off the top layer of raw emotion, reminding yourself that you are going through an undoubted life crisis, and it is therefore to be expected that you feel bad.

If the emotion is not so raw, then turn to this book. If you are watching a friend suffer because of an affair; if you are having an affair yourself and are confused or unhappy; if your partner is having an affair and you need to cope; if you want to end an affair and don't know where to start — in short, when you are ready to grasp what is happening and do something about it — then what I have written will be of use to you.

If you really want to understand the eternal triangle, then read on.

Basic ideas

1 Passion dance

How does it begin? How will it end? How does the eternal triangle develop, from its first beginnings in a glance, through to its consummation in love-making, on to its resolution in parting? Why does it happen?

Most importantly of all, *how* does it happen?

These were the questions I asked as I began to contact the people willing to tell me about their experiences in the eternal triangle. Ruth was the very first person to talk to me. Small and slight, with shoulder-length brown hair, she is now in her early thirties, happily married with one small child. Five years ago, when the man she is now married to was away, she entered into a brief but unforgettable eternal triangle.

Ruth

It lasted for exactly four weeks — three weeks of heaven and a week of hell.

I knew at the time that I was heading into waters more dangerous than I had ever been in before. My partner Greg had just left on a three-week business trip and I was alone. I had no thought of finding someone else, though we had both occasionally taken lovers, short-term, one-night stands about which we were both relaxed. There was no danger; we had a good, sound relationship with not much excitement and a lot of security.

When Greg left at lunchtime, I hung around the house for a while, took a bath, read a book, found to my amazement that I did miss him. We had no children at that time, and there was no one either to worry about me or to care for me. I found I was just a little lonely and I needed company. I rang a friend.

'There's a party on tonight, and you must come.' I remember dressing with care, tight black trousers and a loose white shirt, jewellery, and perfume. I remember seeing myself in the mirror as I left, and laughing at what I saw. Was I really that obvious? I think I knew already that I was looking for an adventure.

The party was a few miles away, a train ride; it was one of those events where you know very few people and lose sight of the ones you know more or less immediately. As I walked through the door, I looked up, and the first thing I saw was this guy coming down the stairs into the hall. My stomach shifted, and at exactly the same moment, I remember thinking very clearly of the exact flight Greg would be taking back, in three weeks' time. I had twenty-one days.

He was tall, very slim, very beautiful. Dark eyes, jeans and a sweater. He looked down and saw me and looked away. I reckoned he was my age or maybe a year or two younger. I couldn't believe he was on his own. When I'd dumped my coat I went to get a drink. I followed him into the kitchen and we ended up pouring wine for each other. Then we began to talk.

We both knew. We didn't know what each other's exact situation was, but we knew how we felt. I didn't even know his name. It was pure physical attraction. I loved Greg and I wanted to stay with him – but this was irresistible.

We talked. He was called Jon, and he was a mature student just finishing an engineering course. He asked about me, my life, all the details. I did tell him I was living with someone, but it was as if there was a double message going on; I was being honest with him on the surface, but my body was being just as honest in a different way.

I was, beyond doubt, picking up similar messages from him. He was single, unattached, though I had the impression of something unresolved somewhere. That was totally irrelevant to what was going on between us, some sort of dance of passion that simply fed off itself. Our fingers would touch as we passed the bottle of wine from one to the other, our voices would drop to just the same pitch as we talked. We were urging each other on just by being with each other.

We ended up dancing, very close, and communicating just as clearly with our bodies as we had with our words. I felt so good, high on the attention and the attraction more than on the wine. When he suggested he drive me back home, I agreed immediately.

It is easy for Ruth to start an affair. Her partner is willing and happy for her to have other relationships. Unlike most of us, she has nothing stopping her going for exactly what she wants.

So it happens. She and Jon are drawn to each other irresistibly in a rising spiral of emotional attraction and physical passion. Each look and each touch pushes them further and further towards a possible affair.

Yet how does it happen? Who creates it?

As all of us who have ever been in love know, there is no simple answer. Who made the first move, who glanced the first glance, who sighed the first sigh. We have no idea – or if we think we do, we can never be quite certain whether this first sign was preceded by one of which we are entirely unaware.

In fact, words and actions are not so important. Crucial human communication happens on a far deeper level. We can control what we say and do – but what really communicates itself to another person, particularly in an area so fraught as the eternal triangle, is the pure emotion. Over this emotion, we may have no control; we may not even be aware we are feeling it until well after it has affected our words and our gestures, and through these the emotions of the person we are with.

So when Ruth agrees to leave with Jon, it is not the words she speaks that tell him she wants him; it is the passion behind the words that he feels and responds to. It is this which moves their relationship on.

We talked very little on the way back. During the party my whole awareness had been focused on how it would be going to bed with Jon. During the drive home, despite everything, I realized that I wasn't prepared yet to go the whole way. That may sound strange, but despite the fact that I was like a bitch on heat, I didn't want to fuck. I didn't know how he would take it, but that was my decision.

When we drew up outside my house, something very strange happened. He stopped the car and looked across at me, and said, 'Can I come in for a coffee?' and then, in the fraction of a second as I hesitated and thought I'd have to get heavy, he said, 'And I do mean a coffee.' I'd really expected him to jump me, and the fact that he didn't actually left me both surprised and relaxed – and I told him so. We were both breathing heavily, even then, but somehow we were holding back – and that was very safe and very nice.

We ended up talking, sprawled on the sofa in my living room, until five o'clock in the morning! I made him bacon and eggs and sent him off again just as day was breaking. We didn't even kiss, but he said he'd call for me again the next evening.

I spent the whole of the following day like an adolescent schoolgirl waiting for her first date. I bathed and washed my hair, did my legs, the lot, and when he arrived I'd had butterflies in my stomach for hours. I kept rushing round the house screaming with delight. It was such a high, such a total high being wanted.

Feeling the way they do, Jon and Ruth's contact could have spiralled up into an instant explosion of sex. That isn't really what Ruth wants. She holds back, and in so doing stabilizes what is happening between them.

The instinct for stability affects every human interaction. We keep things safe, we stop them from changing too fast – and for very good reasons. We know that they could be dangerous, could threaten our emotional stability and therefore our entire lives. Perhaps we also sense that some interactions are important, worth decelerating simply because we want them to last. Through fear and hope, we try to stabilize everything that is emotionally crucial to us. The alternative would be to live our lives as a series of minute-to-minute explosions.

Ruth does have other options. She might have chosen, as the best way of stabilizing her situation and keeping her partnership with Greg emotionally intact, to sleep with Jon, burn out the passion and then never see him again. In fact, when she and Jon approach the point where things might move too fast, she withdraws. She says nothing, but then she does not need to. He knows her feeling and reacts to it, thus saving himself – and their affair. Once given the safety that his drawing back offers, she can trust him enough to move forward again, to allow him into her home and into her life. Had he pushed harder, she might well have fled.

When he arrived that evening, it was as if all the holding back of the day before had made it more intense. As soon as I'd closed the door, I reached for him and we kissed. It was very passionate, but very delicate, an intensity I'd known before with Greg, though not for a while, something very knowledgeable and dangerous.

We ended up on the sofa, with half our clothes on and half off, touching and kissing and licking. After a while, he said, 'Should we go to bed?' and it was then that I said to him that I didn't want to fuck, didn't want to make love with him.

He seemed really cool about that, and I felt safe; so we went to bed. It wasn't even dark, and we lay in the half-light and undressed each other and then held each other under the sheet. Then we touched each other all over, and then we brought each other off. It was amazing. There was just such total communication as to what we wanted, we just seemed to follow each other, like some sort of dance. It wasn't at all 'bouncy', as some men are, with everything happening outside of me, but very much me asking and him giving, him asking and me giving.

When Ruth hesitates, Jon withdraws. By doing this again he gives her the security to take things further.

Let us ask once more who is creating their dynamic. Is it Ruth whose hesitation keeps their relationship from self-destructing, or is it Jon whose distance gives her the safety to come closer? Is it the fact that he is 'good in bed' that makes her so responsive; or her responsiveness that makes him good in bed? Their interactions are totally interdependent, each one a direct result of the one before. In this sense, there is no cause and no effect, no controller and no controlled.

The next three weeks were really weird. I was hardly sleeping, hardly eating, going round in a daze most of the time. I lost half a stone! He had finished his exams, so we'd meet most evenings – and usually just go to bed. We'd come and come and come until we were both exhausted, and laughing at the fact that we still wanted more. And that was true even when we still weren't fucking; we didn't in fact for nearly two weeks. He never ever pressured me, just waited until I was ready.

We'd get up in the middle of the night to eat, and then go back to bed again. We'd go out at dawn and walk round the park. I was a bit scared in case any of the neighbours cottoned on, although it wasn't really that sort of area, so we hardly ever went out near my house. We'd meet at his college, and every week we'd go to the college disco, which was fun. I think he liked to show me off. Sometimes I'd go to his flat, but he only had a single bed and that was awkward. I got on quite well with his flatmates, particularly one woman called Marylynn, although I never said to them directly that I was living with someone else.

The fact that I had a relationship with Greg began to be a problem – or rather it wasn't a problem for me, but it was for Jon, I think. It wasn't that he wanted to spend the rest of his life with me, but I think he was getting involved. I tried to be honest with him. We talked a lot in between the passion, and when he mentioned Greg, I'd say that I loved him and that I thought we'd be together for life. Jon seemed really fine about that, but he checked it out a couple of times, so maybe he wasn't.

The 'something unresolved somewhere' for him turned out to be a woman named Chris, who was on his course and who he'd been out with for a drink a few times. I got the impression that they would have had something going if I hadn't have turned up – and certainly Jon only started talking about her after we had had our first serious conversation about Greg. I tried to help him to talk about it, and I did at one point say something about not wanting to stop him forming a 'proper' relationship. I didn't want him to leave, but I knew it was not my place to do anything but encourage him to find someone who could give him everything he wanted.

I have to be honest – we didn't gel on all levels. We didn't have a lot in common, though he was nice, kind, made me laugh. By the time Greg was due to come back, I knew what I'd known all along. This was not for ever, though I did care for Jon very much.

And we were so good in bed together; it was amazing. We were trying things I'd never done before, and I was coming regularly, which was unheard of for me. I felt sexual in everything I did, I moved differently, talked differently. I was totally intoxicated by it and I wanted it to go on for a long long time.

The three-week period creates an almost perfect stability in the physical side of their affair. On the emotional side, things are very different. Here, Jon is getting involved.

Again, we cannot say how it started, what 'caused' the involvement he feels. Quite simply, somewhere along the line, because of what he felt, or how he reacted to what Ruth felt, it starts to matter to him.

He tests the water by asking about Greg, and Ruth admits that yes, she is committed, and that no, she is not free. She could have lied to him, but she is not that sort of woman. She tells the truth. More importantly, her feelings communicate the truth to Jon in a way that neither of them can deny.

After this, the situation shifts just slightly towards the point where everything will change. For however much we pull a relationship back towards stability, nothing ever remains the same. Things evolve. There is always a slight but inevitable movement in one direction or the other. Think of a spinning top which stays stable on its axis, but inexorably moves across the floor.

Wanting to keep his own safety intact, Jon starts to withdraw. He mentions Chris. This is surely not conscious manipulation; he is probably not even aware of what he is doing. His withdrawal simply happens as a protective response to Ruth's expression of commitment to Greg.

On the physical side of their affair, where her contract with Greg has permitted her ecstatic sexual freedom, Ruth has always felt safe when Jon distanced himself. His holding back has meant she can move towards him. In the case of involvement, things are very different; where Ruth meets Jon's emotional distance, she has to move away, for to move towards him into commitment would be to do what all the sex in the world can never do – betray Greg. So when Jon draws back, Ruth does the same.

That is, as she sees it, her duty to Greg – and her duty to Jon. And when she thinks she is holding him back from a relationship with another woman, she also knows what she must do.

Then it was time for Greg to come back. As the day approached, Jon got a bit moody. I tried to reassure him, but in fact there was no way that we could keep seeing each other as often as we had been doing; things had to change. I said that probably we could meet once a week, and of course we could phone each other.

Our final meeting was on the Thursday when we always went to the college disco; Greg was due back on the Friday.

When I met Jon as usual on that Thursday, from the very beginning something was different. It seemed as if he was

23

trying to pull away, trying to be 'independent'. I missed the closeness, although I felt that I shouldn't go chasing after him. Maybe, too, he wanted some sign from me that I'd realized Greg wasn't so important after all. I couldn't give him that.

As we were sitting there drinking, Jon suddenly looked across the pub and then looked away. I hadn't a clue what had happened – he was obviously a bit shaken. He said that Chris had come in with a group of her friends and had seen him. I was sorry that he felt torn – I really wanted him to get together with her if he wanted to, but I did feel cross that he seemed a bit wary of my reaction. He had no need to be scared of me, but he seemed to think I was going to be angry. I think he picked up my irritation, though I didn't say anything, and he seemed even more shut down after that, which of course just got me more annoyed! It was the first time that had happened, and it was really silly.

It was a strange night; we danced and held each other, and then went back and spent the night together. We both knew it was the last night we'd have for a while, and tried to make it wonderful, but something wasn't quite working.

I did try to be clear with Jon. I really tried to explain to him that if he wanted to go out with Chris, he could tell me and I would understand. I was probably giving him a double message there. I didn't want to lose him, I wanted to carry on seeing him, and I knew that if he did start going out with Chris, they'd want to keep it strictly monogamous. But I did want Jon to get a good relationship for himself, and I was very clear where my priorities lay.

I said I would ring him on the Saturday after Greg got back.

The dynamic repeats itself, and this time the spiral gathers momentum. Jon pulls back more quickly, Ruth more obviously allows him to go. A rising emotion will often push its equivalent response a little higher. As one emotion increases, the other will often follow suit.

There is also a new element to the dynamic. For the first time,

Jon seems wary. Ruth becomes angry; she says nothing, but then she does not need to, and when Jon flinches away, her irritation rises. Within the mutual spiral of attraction, within the equally mutual spiral of withdrawal, is created a new spiral – one of fear and anger that leads inevitably to anger and fear. It is because Jon is scared that Ruth gets annoyed, and it is because Ruth is annoyed that Jon becomes more wary. If he had been less scared ... she might have hugged him. If she had been less angry ... he might have smiled. It might all have changed; the dynamic might have reversed itself.

What happened next was totally unexpected for me, and I still remember it very vividly. Greg came back on Friday, and we had a really good time; we made love almost right away, and we did talk about our respective experiences – everything was really fine.

So on Saturday I rang Jon at his flat. I was really looking forward to talking to him, really happy about Greg coming back, really feeling good about myself.

Jon wasn't in, which was unusual when we'd arranged to have a phone call. I left a message with Marylynn for him to ring me back. We chatted for a while, and she said that she actually hadn't seen him since the day before, but was sure he would ring as soon as he got back. I think that was when my thumbs started pricking. That was Saturday.

There was no word from Jon on Sunday or Monday. I went through hell. What had happened? He must have had my message; maybe he hadn't had time to ring me. I felt just as adolescent as I had when we'd first met, waiting for a phone call. I flipped from being sure that he had got off with Chris, to being certain everything was fine.

On Tuesday evening, about seven o'clock, taking my pride in both hands, I rang his flat again. Marylynn answered. She said that Jon still hadn't been home and everyone was quite worried about him. I was frantic. I was convinced that he had crashed the car or been injured in some way. I was planning to go round, ring his parents, anything. I was also filled with relief that his not getting in touch was nothing to do with me – there was something actually wrong. I told Marylynn that I would ring again at the same time on Wednesday, and she said that she was going to ring the hospitals.

All day Wednesday I was like a cat on hot bricks. I was convinced he was dead. And as soon as I could on Wednesday night, I dialled his number again. Marylynn answered, and the minute I heard her voice I realized that nothing was wrong – and everything was over.

'Oh, hi. I did hear from Jon. He rang this afternoon and when I told him you'd been in touch he said to tell you he's OK. He's been staying with a friend and that he'll write to you.' She was desperately embarrassed and obviously pitied me a great deal. I just felt humiliated.

A few days later I got the letter I expected. Over the weekend, Jon and Chris had got together. She had, he said, 'been very sad that you and I had been seeing each other, and in view of that and the fact that Chris and I have a relationship now, I think it is best if we don't meet again. Have a good time. Jon.'

I was totally enraged. I felt that I'd been let down in the worst possible way. I also began to realize just how much I missed Jon, how much I liked his love-making and how good I felt when I was around him.

I do despise him now, not for finishing with me, but for the way he did it. I think he could have been clear about what was happening, could have rung me to tell me what was going on.

I know that some people will feel I 'have no right' to demand anything of him, but I still feel I was right to be clear with him about my love for Greg. We did have a relationship, Jon and I, and I would have liked not to be regarded as someone who was just having a fling. It wasn't going to last for a lifetime, it wasn't 'serious', but it was good, and I still can't forget him, or forgive him.

The dynamic which ends the relationship is as interdependent and as mutually created as the initial one that landed them in bed together.

It is because Jon withdraws just slightly at the start of their affair that Ruth responds with heightened passion. Later, it is because he withdraws emotionally that she feels she must let him go. It is because she lets him go that he feels he must withdraw. This spiral must self-destruct and it does.

Every human relationship has a change-point, or a series of change-points, evolving directly from what has gone before. It might not be a break-up; it might be a row, a love-making, a further commitment, a marriage, a child. When things evolve, however, either by a rising spiral of good feelings, or by a rising spiral of bad feelings, our relationships have to tip over into a new configuration.

Things might have gone differently for Jon and Ruth, but only if they could have stepped outside the dynamic. Yet this is unlikely. In reality, Ruth would not, in the end, have chosen to commit herself less to Greg. Jon might have been willing to stay for a while, but he would not have stayed for ever. The affair reached its logical conclusion, its inevitable change-point.

Why does the ending happen as it does, so suddenly and without communication? To understand, we must remember the previous spiral of anger and fear – and when we do, Jon's withdrawal seems not sudden at all, but the direct result of the complex interactions that have gone before.

Over the final weekend, some kind of chance meeting with Chris undoubtedly created a fresh possibility for Jon. Jon opts for this, withdrawing finally from Ruth and entering a new dynamic with Chris. He cannot go back and tell Ruth, for in their relationship there is now an additional spiral of fear. Scared of Ruth's possible anger, Jon pulls back even from contacting her, seeks safety and reassurance with Chris and finally finishes the affair by the ultimate disengagement, a letter. That way, he is completely safe.

Ruth is left distraught. She had thought that by giving Jon freedom, she was honouring her friendship with him. She no doubt feels she had no choice other than to remain loyal to Greg. How was she to know that Jon would end it all so dishonestly?

When Jon learns of her anger, he must surely feel equally disturbed. He had thought that by withdrawing, he was giving Ruth the space she needed. He no doubt feels he had no choice other than to get together with Chris when the opportunity arose. How was he to know that Ruth would find this such a betrayal?

Of course, things could have been different. If Ruth had not felt so loving towards Greg, she might have moved towards Jon at some point and forestalled their break-up. If Jon had not felt so loving towards Ruth, he would not have felt the need to move away once Greg was back. Had Chris not have wanted Jon, then maybe he would have had nowhere to withdraw to. Had Greg not been so supportive to Ruth, she might never even have registered Jon's presence as he walked down the stairs . . .

The images that come through Ruth's story, the new perspective it offers us, can be seen like this. Picture two points, a little way apart, representing Ruth and Jon beginning to create their relationship. From Ruth to Jon there is a curve of emotion, linking her to him, affecting him directly with her affection, her sexuality, her desire. From Jon to Ruth, in return, there is a similar curve of emotion, linking him to her, affecting her directly with his affection, his sexuality, his desire.

The curves of emotion are a loop, a mutual and never-ending spiral of feeling, Ruth's desire creating Jon's arousal, his slight withdrawal creating her sexual security and enthusiasm. The loop moves slowly like a spinning top across time, sometimes stabilizing as feelings settle, then shifting as one emotion moves the other on. Eventually, as the relationship evolves to a change point, the loop breaks down completely and each of them takes up new positions, Jon with Chris, and Ruth in her original relationship with Greg.

To begin to understand the dynamic of any relationship, see it in this way: a loop, a spiral, a movement, a change.

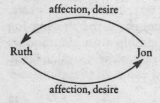

2 Duet for three

You may already have begun to analyse your own situation in terms of the ideas in Ruth's story. You may already be realizing that every time you argue, every time you make love, you are also reflecting the patterns explored there.

You, too, are in emotional loops with others; your feelings affect theirs, and their feelings affect yours through the medium of words and actions. Your loop of emotion may remain stable as you settle into a regular interaction, or it may evolve — because you become more involved with your partner, or because you become more disillusioned with each other. Somewhere along the line, suddenly or imperceptibly, in days, months or years, a change will occur. You will find that you are relating in a new way: more committed, less friendly, totally antagonistic, totally besotted. Because of what has been happening in your particular dynamic (or, of course, because of what has happened in other areas of your life) something has shifted and the relationship has moved on.

It is amazing to watch how perspectives can change when you start to view the world in terms of these patterns. When you stop seeing interactions in terms of words and actions only, but rather in terms of communicating emotions, then suddenly those agonizing and incomprehensible arguments begin to make sense. 'What did I say?' is not important; 'What was I feeling?' allows you to understand what happened next.

When you stop seeing interactions in terms of one person only affecting the other, but instead in terms of a mutual and never-ending loop, then all at once you can see that you are an equal participant, influencing your relationship just by your emotional presence. 'He *made* me angry' seems inaccurate; 'We created the row together' is far nearer the truth.

When you can stop seeing beginnings, endings, rows and reconciliations not as sudden, inexplicable events, but rather as the result of an ever-moving and evolving dynamic, then they suddenly become comprehensible and predictable. 'It just happened out of the blue' is replaced by 'Now I see the pattern, it all makes sense'.

Acts of God can still happen – but where your interaction is concerned, you can begin to understand what is happening between the two of you.

Or the three of you.

For everything that happens between two happens between three. The rules are the same. The dynamics follow the same pattern. The only difference in what happens is that there are three relationships involved, not just one.

Time and time again, as I spoke to interviewees, I realised that the 'key' interaction, the affair on which I was supposed to be focusing, was only one of three. In an eternal triangle there are relationships between not just two, but three people. If a woman has a partner and a lover, she has a link with both – and most people would admit that both will affect her. What I found is that both the partner and the lover of the person having an affair also have a relationship with each other. Whether or not they ever meet, they affect each other deeply through their common link with their mutual love.

If you still believe that words and gestures are the most crucial elements of interaction, then it may be difficult to accept that these two people can have an emotional relationship with each other. Yet if a husband is angry, and through his anger makes his wife feel guilty, then that guilt will inevitably affect her interaction with her lover. Perhaps she will now respond to her lover with resentment, perhaps with more reassurance or more gratitude. Whatever happens, in some way her feelings will be altered, her relationship with him will be changed, and therefore her lover will be affected by her husband.

Picture then, instead of the two-pointed loop in Ruth's story, a three-pointed loop – the triangle. Each point of the triangle is one of its participants: the person who is having an affair, their partner, their lover. Each of them is joined to the other two points of the triangle by the emotion that passes between them, a two-way loop of feeling from and to, to and from. Of course, each of these loops is identical to the two-way loop described in Ruth's story, with an emotion-to-emotion response, a pull towards stability, a drift towards change, a constant evolution of the dynamic.

So there are now three sets of interlocking relationships: partner and partner, partner and lover, lover and partner. The interaction between lover and partner may be indirect – as I have just pointed out, they may relate only through their mutual love – but it will be there.

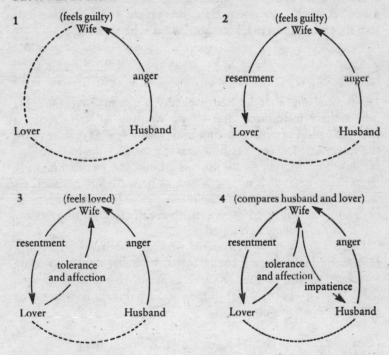

The dynamic is complex. What either one of the couple feels will affect the other – and that will affect the lover. A sudden change in the lover's emotions will have spin-offs for both partners, and their interaction may change radically. If the relationship between a man and his mistress suddenly shifts, then inevitably his wife will feel the impact, because he will transmit totally different feelings. If a woman has a sudden shift in her attitude to her husband, then inevitably her lover will be affected, because she will be feeling a totally new way.

In your eternal triangle – or the one you know of, perhaps – a similar dynamic may be happening. Together, each influencing the other, you may create a situation of stability. Together, passing emotion from person to person, you may move the interaction towards a change point. Together, by creating shifts in each other, you will also create the patterns of withdrawal or bonding that eventually bring the triangle to its conclusion. Together, with your interaction, you create a recognizable pattern that allows you to understand what is happening.

James

James rang me after he had seen my letter in *Time Out*. He immediately introduced himself as wanting to 'talk about a triangle', and I arranged to ring him back a few days later to do the interview. I never met him, never saw what he looked like. He described himself as tall and well-built, but I knew him only from his voice, which was soft and, at first, slightly hesitant. As we delved more deeply into the memories of his relationship, he began to remember, to open out, to recall clearly and precisely just how the triangle developed.

James's story is of a triangle which created a partnership. James and his partner Jeanette began by being unable to come together, simply because their emotional dynamic reinforced their staying apart. When James took a lover, however, the dynamic began to shift.

I first met Jeanette about six years ago. We were doing a teacher training course at Oxford, and when the course started we were both based in the same school doing our pre-teaching practice. Jeanette was attractive, small and slim with long, dark hair, but it wasn't really a physical attraction at first.

When we finished teaching practice and went back to do the

college course, we stayed friends. Jeanette and I would spend time together, watch dancing together; we had a lot in common, though the relationship still didn't develop into anything more intimate. On the very last day of the course, we went for a long walk among the trees. We talked and talked for hours, and I did put my arm around her, but that was all. I think that by that time we both knew there was an attraction there, but we were both nervous; I, certainly, was very unsure just how attractive I was to women. We didn't talk about what was happening, didn't explore our emotions, just parted company for the summer.

For James and Jeanette, the dynamic is a constant holding back. This is what creates their stability, what keeps them apart. Again, it is not the words or actions that are crucial; when James and Jeanette are walking among the trees, it is primarily their nervousness that stops their relationship from developing. It is James who lacks the confidence to move forward, and his emotion transmits itself to Jeanette. It is her holding back that reinforces his lack of confidence. It is his lack of confidence which reinforces her holding back.

I got a teaching job the following year and there I met Bindu. She was a teacher at the school, very, very beautiful and physically fit. I was attracted to her from the first time I saw her, and I was sure she felt the same.

One day, she invited me to lunch in the nearby pub. We sat talking and drinking, and I remember that other teachers from the school came up to chat to us but then went away. Perhaps they realized that we wanted to be alone together; I certainly wasn't aware of it, but maybe we were giving off that kind of signal.

We got into the car to go back to school, and, all of a sudden, Bindu leaned over and kissed me. It was an incredibly strong experience, more powerful than anything I had ever felt before, and very unexpected. We kissed for a while and then had to go back to work, but we arranged to meet after school;

she came back to my flat and we kissed and held each other. Eventually, before we'd made love, she left.

I was stunned because it was so incredibly intense, of a physical intensity that I'd never experienced. In the past I'd got to know people before I'd gone out with them, often over two or three months or even longer. So something that happened so quickly and so intensely was quite new to me.

I've asked myself whether, if Bindu hadn't made the first move, I would have done. I'm sure the answer is no.

The same James who holds back with Jeanette moves forward when he is with Bindu. For with a different person, interacting with different emotions, James responds differently. It is Bindu who makes the first move, but when she shows him by doing so just what she feels for him, then his self-confidence soars. Her eagerness finds an answering eagerness in him.

The result is a change in James. He cannot help but respond to Bindu with an intensity of his own, cannot help but join her in the loop of emotion. What he feels from Bindu gives him a new sense of his own worth; it cannot but transform the emotions he communicates to others.

I rang Jeanette. I felt that I ought to tell her what was happening between Bindu and I, because it might affect what there was or wasn't happening between us. I felt she had a right to know, even though nothing had really started with her, and even though she herself seemed to think it strange I was telling her.

A few days later, something amazing happened. Jeanette wrote to me. In her letter, she said that my relationship with Bindu had precipitated something inside her, and prompted her to realize that she actually wanted to have a relationship with me and had been nervous of telling me. Now she was afraid it would never happen, so she wanted to speak out.

I rang her back, and she came round to see me. I was living in a shared house at the time with three other people, but they were out. We sat for a while downstairs in the communal living room and talked 'round' the subject, carefully avoiding it; she'd bought a new jacket and trousers and I'd recently bought some new clothes too, so we chatted about those. Gradually, we started talking about how we both felt, the strange last meeting in Oxford when nothing had happened, and how we had both wanted something to happen . . . then we started kissing. Then my housemates came in.

We moved upstairs to my bedroom and carried on kissing, becoming very physical, although we still kept our clothes on. Jeanette was using a diaphragm for contraception at the time, and she said she'd thought about bringing it with her, but hadn't. So we didn't sleep together, but when she left we agreed to meet the following weekend.

James's emotions have altered, and inevitably his relationship with Jeanette has to change. His new self-confidence shows itself in the way he rings her, approaches her, even though neither of them are sure what he is saying. Their dynamic destabilizes, a further change-point occurs. In response to James's altered emotions, Jeanette is able to contact new ones of her own.

The fear that she might lose James and the deep desire she feels for him did not show themselves before. Now she not only feels them, but is able to communicate them. James responds, she moves closer, and they enter a slower and more thoughtful version of the arousal spiral that Bindu and James are also engaged in.

Is it Bindu who has created this? Certainly she has not done so consciously or deliberately; we suspect that nothing has been further from her mind. Nevertheless, by altering James's feelings, she has set in motion a train of events. It is this that, transmitted through James, creates in Jeanette the emotional resources to get what she wants. Bindu and Jeanette have their own significant interaction, even though they have never met.

Meanwhile, it was half-term from school, and so I hadn't seen Bindu at all. But immediately after half-term, she came round to my flat again for a second time. We at once became very passionate and aroused. She looked at me and said 'Aren't we going to talk first?' I just said 'No.' I took all her clothes off, we made love and it was wonderful.

After that things settled into a pattern. I would see Bindu after school maybe three or four nights a week. She would quite often stay until mid-evening, eight o'clock or so, and we would make love virtually the whole time. It was extremely intense.

I would see Jeanette at weekends, and again the relationship was incredibly physical; we would spend almost all the time in bed. Never before, and never since have I made love so much – some weeks all my spare time was spent making love. I was extremely happy in the situation. I am fairly highly sexed, I think, and it was probably the only time in my life that I made love as much as I really wanted to, as much as my body wanted to.

I wasn't tempted to compare them as lovers, although there were differences. Bindu was about twenty-six, small and slim with long, coarse dark hair, physically very fit and slightly muscular. I like muscular women, not body-builders, but women who are fit as swimmers or divers are. Bindu also did a lot of yoga, so she was very supple. She was, in fact, far and away the most attractive woman I've ever made love with, before or since. She was very free in bed; we did whatever we felt like, with no negative feelings, no drawing back. She could really let go, and would move a lot and scream a lot. It was natural to go on and on, have more and more, make love again and again and again.

Jeanette was thirty-two. She was never a physically sporty person, so she was never as well toned as Bindu, not nearly as firm. We would hold each other and touch each other, stroke and kiss a lot; not so much sheer love-making, more sensuality. She was a little more reserved in bed than Bindu was – but not a lot.

There was no conflict for me; it seemed perfectly right to be sleeping with both of them and to be honest with them about what was happening. There was a natural break in that I saw Bindu during the week and couldn't see her at weekends, and I saw Jeanette at weekends but not during the week. I think the two relationships were compartmentalized, so there were no tears at all. Bindu knew about Jeanette but definitely wasn't jealous of her; she was married, so in a sense she couldn't be jealous. I think Jeanette was a bit jealous at first, but she felt that she couldn't be because my relationship with Bindu had helped us get together in the first place.

I found out that Bindu was married after we first made love. I met her husband a few times at staff parties, but I didn't feel upset in any way because he was there; I knew the relationship she and I had. Equally, I certainly wasn't frightened by him; other males don't really threaten me at all.

And I'm sure Bindu's relationship with her husband was never in danger. She came from a traditional family with very strong cultural and religious ties; all hell would have been let loose if the marriage had broken up. Anyway, I'm sure that wasn't what she wanted. Her husband didn't know what was going on, though he had enough signals, because she would stay out until mid-evening with me three or four evenings a week. I don't know what she told him. Maybe he chose to turn a blind eye.

I don't think Bindu's sexual relationship with her husband was all that good. I went to a party at her house a while after we'd finished the relationship, and it seemed to me that they were very rich in material terms, but there was no spark in her life. I think she got the spark she wanted from relationships outside her marriage. She had had an affair with another teacher the year before I arrived, and I know that she also had a relationship with another of the teachers after we'd finished. Maybe she needed affairs to stay happy.

The dance continues. Then it stabilizes, with each person's emotion responding to those of the others. For a whole half-term,

James makes love with Bindu during the week and Jeanette at weekends. Neither of them demands that he stop seeing the other, neither of them withdraws from the situation. For his part, James is contented, confident, secure.

Why does neither woman object? The answers James gives seem to be realistic ones; neither, for their own reasons, believes they can object. For Bindu, asking James to give up Jeanette would be a statement of commitment she is not prepared to make. Jeanette, we suspect, knows that a similar request would push the dynamic too far, too fast. She opts for stability, and bides her time.

All dynamics must evolve. The movement might have come from Bindu's husband, demanding that his wife stop her affairs. But despite fairly clear signals, he does not challenge her, and we can never be sure whether he consciously knew but accepted the facts, or did not know and chose to remain unknowing.

Bindu might have become more involved with James – but all the signs are that Bindu, like Ruth, is locked in her prior relationship. She may repeat the cycle of affairs over and over, but she will never renege on her commitment. And James knows this. If he had ever thought of moving towards her, he would have been instantly aware that such a move was impossible.

James might have grown tired of both women, but in the short time span of the affairs that is unlikely to happen. For the moment, he is happy, he cares for them both in different ways. But the situation cannot remain stable for ever. It must move. The way it does shift is, in hindsight, inevitable.

We carried on as we were for a whole half-term, perhaps six or eight weeks. Then, just before Christmas, I was spending the weekend with Jeanette and we talked quite a lot about what was happening. Over the weeks there had been a growing feeling that things were getting quite serious between us, so I asked her if she wanted me to give up Bindu.

She said yes.

So I agreed that I would. I meant it and I kept to it. I feel trust and truth are the most important things in a relationship, so if

I do say something, I won't go back on it. I didn't want to give up Bindu, but I had promised I would, so I did.

I know that Jeanette saw it all as a sign that we were growing closer. She always spoke of that weekend, in particular, as being a good one. She had felt that she had no right to ask me to give Bindu up, but when I offered, and agreed to do so, she was very happy indeed.

Then I was faced with breaking the news to Bindu, which I did on the very last day of term. We were having a staff party and I drew her to one side and said I wanted to talk to her. We both went through to the Staff Room, where it was quiet, and I told her then. I said that Jeanette and I were getting quite serious, and that I didn't feel it was fair on Jeanette to continue seeing her.

Bindu was shocked and upset. I don't think she'd seen it coming at all. I was very upset too, though I didn't show it. But there were no tears, no rows. It was almost functional; I told her, we sat there for a while, and then we left.

So the eternal triangle ended. In a way it had to, although for a while afterwards I still had 'that feeling' in the pit of my stomach every time I saw Bindu. But I don't think we could ever have had a future together; both of us knew from the start that it was something that wouldn't last. I did see a long-term future with Jeanette. I knew I wanted that, and our relationship lasted for several years afterwards.

It was a good time for me, that time of the eternal triangle. It gave me a lot more confidence, and I stopped wondering what on earth a woman could see in me. I have very happy memories of that time, even now.

In the end, there are no surprises, no chance events that disrupt the inevitable progress of the dynamic. James has always been drawn towards Jeanette, has moved closer and closer to her throughout the half-term.

Had she not been able to justify to herself James's affair, then she might well have pushed him away when he approached. As it is, she wanted both his company and his love-making. When he moved towards her, she responded and they spiralled together into a closeness which increases with each passing weekend ... and climaxes with James's offer of monogamy. This new change-point is a natural result of his movement towards Jeanette, away from Bindu. It is a strong statement of contact, the direct opposite of the disengagement of Jon and Ruth. Jeanette's happiness at the offer draws equal delight from James, binding them even closer, making it even more certain that his relationship with Bindu will end.

Of course he regrets the ending; he is leaving the most attractive woman he has ever made love with. But his bond with Jeanette grows, must have grown or otherwise the dynamic would have tilted back again. He remains faithful and gradually the feeling for Bindu dies away.

Bindu is shocked when the end comes. She is not able to move closer, but she has not expected the withdrawal quite so soon. Does she realize the role she herself has played in creating James's partnership with Jeanette? Does she realize that by raising his self-confidence she has enabled him to enter another relationship, and that by remaining in her marriage she has encouraged him to commit himself to that relationship? She is sad to lose James, and, like Ruth, she probably mourns the loss of her lover. However, she soon enters another liaison, repeating again the dynamic she had with James in a new, and equally temporary, partnership.

James's story highlights the complex dynamic of the triangle, with its three, linked, emotional loops. In human interaction, everyone is totally interdependent; in three-way relationships, we are linked in three interlocking associations with two other people, whose dual emotions combine with ours to produce the whole.

If we enter into a triangle we start it because we are responding to, or reacting against, fleeing from, or moving towards, the emotions that we feel from others. It is not always that your spouse rejects and your lover makes you welcome. Perhaps, like James, you feel confident enough through one affair to make the first move in another. Perhaps you feel enough pressure – or enough love – from your spouse to accept him or her looking for a lover.

If we maintain a triangle, we do so because of the complex blend of emotions from all those around us that makes it more worthwhile to do so than to stop. When James feels loved and accepted by both Bindu and Jeanette, he simply wants to carry on. When your lover finds you sexually exciting and your husband is off sex, you can find all the reasons in the world to carry on an affair. When your wife seems happier because she is taking a lover, you can sometimes find it acceptable to turn a blind eye.

If we destabilize a triangle, then we end it because we are pulled or pushed into a new way of relating by the emotions of two other people. James moves towards Jeanette and is welcomed, moves away from Bindu and meets little resistance because her commitment is elsewhere; the result is inevitable. If your husband rejects and your lover supports, then you will probably move towards your lover. If your husband supports and your lover demands, then you will probably move towards your husband. If your husband complains and your lover blames, then you may well withdraw from both, in order to survive.

This may all sound as if all our actions are dictated by others. The stories in this book show that nothing could be further from the truth; the emotional loop is truly interdependent. Everyone is affected by everyone else, and the emotions of those around us are created by our emotions, just as surely as ours are created by theirs. People do bring their own personalities to every interaction and so individual reactions differ – but each response is created directly by the previous emotion, and each emotion is created by the previous response. What we felt before is the direct result of the feeling we responded to, and the feeling we responded to is the direct result of the one we communicated. The loop goes round and round, the start point is never really identifiable, the real initiator is impossible to pin down.

Whatever happens between two, can happen between three.

3 Let's play blame

As you read the stories in this book, and as you link the explanations of them back to your own situation, you may find yourself hampered in your understanding and appreciation of them by negative emotions. You may be mentally criticizing those who are in an eternal triangle, you may be regarding as essentially flawed relationships which are based on three-way love.

Time and again, as I spoke to interviewees, they told me that such negative emotions were the main block they had found to really understanding their situation. They were angry at partners' reactions, they criticized lovers' behaviour, they berated themselves for feeling bad about other people. 'I have never blamed so many people, so often . . .' said one interviewee.

I came to realize that in affairs, blame is not a subsidiary emotion. Eternal triangles are founded on a bedrock of blame, and it inevitably prevents us, whether as participants or onlookers, from seeing clearly what is going on. In other contexts, even in other kinds of relationships, we can often appreciate the total picture, see things from other people's point of view, and hence analyse and act upon the complete situation. In the eternal triangle, our entire background and culture prime us to presuppose something is wrong, to find the culprit, point the finger and then blame – thus focusing all our attention on one person, one action, one small section of the picture.

That we should want to point the finger of blame is understandable. As I mentioned in the Introduction to this book, an affair is a direct challenge to many of our social norms, so even if we have never experienced one, it can make us feel threatened and defensive.

Equally, if an affair has been a painful experience for you, what else is there to do but to try to find a reason for it? What easier way is there than to say that the situation is essentially wrong, as are the people involved, and to judge them accordingly and to try to alter the situation by blaming the participants? It is not just 'abandoned spouses' who need to talk of 'fault'. If you are the partner who has fallen in love elsewhere, you will find reasons why your partner 'made you' leave. If you are the lover, you will swing between alternately blaming your beloved's spouse and then blaming your beloved. In all three positions of the triangle, you may well end up blaming yourself.

Why do we bother blaming? We do so for one very logical reason; we have been taught to. At our mother's knee – or rather, over it – we were shown that if we broke a social rule, this was a bad thing and we got punished. Internalizing these lessons as we all do, we quickly learned that if a social rule gets broken someone is at fault and must be punished. That way, the offender won't do it again.

The eternal triangle breaks all the social rules and, of course, triggers off our belief that something is very wrong and some individual somewhere must be punished. If it is we who seem to be at fault, perhaps we punish ourselves mentally with the instrument of self-blame, rather than hitting ourselves physically as our parents once hit us. When we think it is others who are at fault, we consider it our job to punish them – and as it is no longer acceptable to stone adulterers to death, we punish them instead by blaming them, either in words or in our thoughts.

Certainly, as an immediate reaction when we are frightened or angry, blaming someone is a satisfactory way to ease the pain. 'I didn't want to be told to calm down, or to see things reasonably,' said one man whose wife had left him to live with her lover. 'I just wanted to feel as bad as possible about both of them.'

Blame may be satisfying, but is it always appropriate? Although affairs break the social rules of many people in Britain in the 1990s, it should be remembered that in other countries and at other times, affairs are and were socially acceptable. On the evidence of the interviews I held, I would question whether blame is an appropriate response to adultery.

First, I challenge the assumption that affairs themselves are necessarily always a bad thing. For many of the people I met, their involvement in 'adultery' may or may not have been moral, but it was beneficial. Many of my interviewees, to my surprise, said they realized in hindsight that, whether they were 'lover', 'adulterer' or 'betrayed spouse', an affair was the best thing that could have happened to them. Perhaps it highlighted needs they were ignoring, perhaps it enabled them to end a pointless relationship, perhaps it raised their self-esteem or that of their partner, or perhaps it acted as a stepping-stone to new things. It became impossible for me, after a while, to regard affairs with the blanket condemnation that I had hitherto felt.

Secondly, I challenge the appropriateness of blame; because very often it causes nothing but trouble for ourselves. We have been taught – also over our mother's knee – that it is bad to criticize others; so if we blame someone, then we may feel guilty about doing so. Several interviewees reported feeling worse about their own negative feelings than about the events themselves that had triggered the blame in the first place. Blame so often ends up as self-blame.

Thirdly, even if we do hold that adultery is always wrong, then blame is by no means a foolproof way of applying social sanctions against it. Spanking rarely stops children raiding the biscuit tin, and blaming rarely stops adults having affairs. Many of the people I spoke to wanted their partners or lovers to change what they were doing – making love, not making love, being jealous, playing hard to get. Few interviewees had achieved this aim simply by feeling bad about the other person or their actions. The bottom line is that we cannot make other people *feel* the way we want them to by guilt-tripping them into doing so. Blaming may, through fear, get others to speak or act a certain way, but it will not change their emotions and so the words and actions are meaningless.

If blaming is only occasionally an appropriate response, if it fails to take into account affairs as a positive change-point in a relationship, if in the long term it makes us feel bad, if it is only marginally effective, if it narrows our perspective on a problem, then perhaps it is time to try a new approach? But what is a more appropriate response?

The answer has to lie in stepping back and being able to see the total dynamic in any situation. The whole idea of emotional loops means that you can never say anyone 'caused' a situation and therefore that anyone is at fault. In all my many interviews, in every triangle I explored, there was no one single 'cause', no one person who by themselves was a starting point for the situation. Everyone together created the outcome by their interlocking dynamic. The interplay of emotion was such that it was impossible to say that any one individual 'caused' the triangle to happen. For if emotional interactions are truly interdependent, then your feelings (and therefore your words and actions) are a direct result of mine anyway. So why should I blame you? As my feelings (and words and actions) are a direct result of yours, why should you blame me? As every emotional response is 'caused' by the one before it, who originally caused what? How far back do we wish to go to lay the blame, and which of us should cast the first stone?

To those of you who are concerned that such a model offers no social sanctions to provide security and to enforce the social norms, let me offer reassurance. All relationships, including eternal triangles, have better methods of applying social sanctions than blaming, for they have built-in ways to encourage people to behave one way and discourage them from behaving another. Every human being in the world uses 'sanctions' and 'rewards', usually unconsciously, to affect other people and the way they act. A baby's gurgle of glee, a lover's sigh of pleasure, a partner's smile of happiness – they all encourage the recipient to give more, to repeat whatever action has caused such satisfaction. Conversely, the cry, the frown, the grimace, however unconscious, will discourage. We know this, and in the first euphoria of love, we use it happily and effectively to spiral the relationship upwards into ecstasy.

We may then ask why such 'rewards' and 'sanctions' do not always get the results they want. When problems strike, when the eternal triangle puts strain on every interaction between us, we often forget to look at what works. All too often, the effect our actions have is the direct opposite of the result we want, and we end up shouting our partner not into submission but into resistance or placating our lover not into compliance but into dominance.

If we learn to understand relationships by looking at the dynamics they involve, we will begin to see just how we influence other people's behaviour and how they influence ours. This gives us a far more subtle and effective way to apply social sanctions than merely blaming – it allows us to choose not only to nag an erring partner, but to meet their needs, not only to tell a lover how wrong they are, but also to create the situation where they can find out what is right.

The two interviews that follow show two very different perspectives on blame and the issues it raises. Both interviews demonstrate how affairs can be seen as either destructive or beneficial, depending on our viewpoint and on the ultimate outcome. Both also demonstrate that it is possible to choose neither to blame others nor to blame yourself – and to be happier and more fulfilled as a result. Neither interviewee uses blame as a sanction – but people in both of the triangles attempt to persuade or pressurise others, and in each case their ultimate intention fails because they are using inappropriate means – their emotional pressure simply doesn't work.

Clare

Clare contacted me through a mutual friend. We met at lunch time in a tiny square in the City of London, and ate our sandwiches on a bench under trees, laughing every time someone passed and stared at the tape recorder.

Clare is slim, tall and redheaded. A successful business woman, she works in the City, is just married, and full of confidence. Her story, however, is one that many women would dread – of discovering that her partner has a lover. But for Clare, the issues were not so clear cut.

I suppose the story of my eternal triangle starts when I began my relationship with Michael. We were working in the same office in Liverpool. He was dark, with brown skin, slightly shorter than I am and quite homely looking. He certainly wasn't my physical type.

At first, I wasn't attracted to him at all. He came for a meal to the house I shared with some other women. He brought another guy, and there were eight women there; it was a very funny situation. But I didn't really notice him then. We followed that up with meals at his place, but nothing happened for a while; I knew he was courting me because he would take a lot of care in the way he dressed, would glance at me sometimes in a certain way – but he was very discreet.

I first realized that he cared when we drove up the coast one night in his car. We were talking intimately and I told him that six months earlier I had had an abortion. He got upset and said, 'I don't like it when you talk about things that have hurt you in the past. I care about you a lot.' That was what showed me that it wasn't just friendship; we walked along the shore arm in arm then, and although nothing was said, I think I stayed the night with him, maybe that night, or maybe very soon after.

I have to say that Michael was very good to me. He was gentle, kind, attentive. He helped me when I was depressed. I'm sure he loved me. It was an irresistible combination. He got on very well with my family, and in fact acted as a catalyst to help me have a better relationship with my parents. I had a lot of sharp edges in those days and he protected people from those. In some ways he suppressed me, but actually he helped me a great deal.

Nevertheless, it was always a very low-key relationship, a sort of habit. I didn't fancy him much; he was great as a friend, but as a lover I didn't feel passionate about him, never got much out of sex.

For him, things were much more serious. He said from the start that he wanted to marry me, to settle down, have children, share a future together – and that was absolutely not what I wanted. What I wanted was to change the world. It drove me crazy. Every six weeks or so we would talk, and I would tell him I was not settling down with him. He would stay quiet about it for a while, but then mention it again; he simply didn't believe me.

Then one summer about four years after we'd started going out with each other, Michael was away on holiday with his sister, and I went off on a course.

During the course, I made a change within myself. We were doing a lot of self-development work, a lot of exercises and games and counselling about feeling good about ourselves. And I did. I remember one particular occasion I suddenly felt very, very different. I made a decision that I had enough space in my life to have a child, and that I loved myself. I realized all at once that I didn't need Michael, and I didn't need him to love me in order to survive.

Then I literally turned around and noticed in the same group this absolutely wonderful man. He was delicious: physically perfect, taller than me, with curly grey hair, beautiful eyes and the softest, most delicious Irish accent. There was a kind of mystery about him. His name was Joe, and I fell in love with him all at once.

We spent a lot of time together during that weekend. We went for long walks and talked, wandering along country lanes and looking at the stars. I remember he had a wonderful smell about him.

I thought at the time that Joe was unattached. He told me that he had had a relationship, but it was on the way out, and he was very clear that he wanted a common future with me. In actual fact, he was still involved with his partner Brigitte, and she was at the workshop. I wondered what the funny vibes from her were, but didn't know. It only gradually dawned on me that his relationship with her was not the 'end of the affair' thing he had told me it was. If I'd known that at the start, I would have walked away – and he knew that.

When I really got to think over that aspect of things, I judged him as a real bugger. In hindsight, I wonder. When I was with him, I was convinced that Michael would understand what was going on between Joe and I – but I was proved totally wrong. It was as if, when I was with Joe, I could see real possibilities, which in fact didn't work out in the cold light of day. I now believe that the same thing happened for him – that when he was with me, he actually did believe that his relationship with Brigitte was over and that we had a future together.

I did fall in love. I had never felt like that before. But I didn't make love with Joe right away. We slept in the same bed, were naked together, and we did help each other to come, but I didn't make love with him. I did hope that I could love both of them, but I wouldn't have deceived Michael.

In fact, during that course was the first time that I knew that I loved Michael; before, I had wondered. I suddenly realised that although I felt passionate about Joe, I had a very deep friendship with Michael, four years of getting on with him, of oneness. I remember looking up at the sun one day and thinking that wherever Michael was on holiday, we were both under the same sun.

When Michael got back from his holiday, we went for a long walk in a forest and I started to tell him what had happened. I felt uncomfortable about doing it, but I was still very clear and happy from being with Joe. Anyway, I wouldn't have deceived Michael for anything. I said, 'I've got something to tell you. I've met a man, and I love him and want to be with him. I know I love you too.' He was quiet for a long while; he seemed quite amazed. He asked me all the details, what we had done, whether we had slept together or not.

And then something really shocking happened. Michael said, 'I have something I need to tell you, too. For the past six months, I've been making love with a girl from work.'

I was completely shattered, not because he had had an affair, but because I'd known he was having one and he had denied it. Things had made me suspicious; he had suddenly not allowed me to go anywhere near his office, pick him up from or go into the pub near his office with him. And he'd done some new things in bed, things I hadn't taught him. I said to him, 'I'm really suspicious; I think you're sleeping with someone else,' and he had denied it completely.

In fact, he had regretted it and had finished the affair, but I had known. For it had affected our relationship – and one of the really interesting things was that it had altered it for the better. Things had changed between us: about six months ago, things had got a great deal better, and I know now that it was because he had taken a lover. Michael was very demanding sexually; I felt cuddly towards him, but often I didn't want to make love and I found it all quite heavy. But then things changed, he wasn't so demanding and as a result our whole relationship got better. That may be why I didn't pursue it, why I didn't want to expose it; things were actually better because he was having an affair.

We did row, particularly about me and Joe rather than about his affair. I wasn't all that upset in fact, and Michael was amazed that I was so cool about it. I wasn't particularly angry with Michael; equally I didn't go rushing off to Joe.

After that, things happened very quickly. Michael decided to put everything into his relationship with me; it might have seemed that that would have made things better between us, but in fact it didn't. There was a shift in his attitude. He became a lot more intense, a lot more focused on me. All of a sudden his expectations got higher. Our relationship couldn't survive that – and it didn't.

When I missed my period, we both became convinced that I was pregnant. That was a turning point. It became very clear to me that if I was going to have the child, I would have it on my own. I didn't actually need or want Michael to help bring up my child, though I did see him as visiting and playing a part in our lives. When he finally realized this, he also realized that I wasn't seeing a future with him at all, and there was no point in our having a relationship. He hadn't actually seen that before; in fact he said to me that he had never believed me when I told him so. It was then he decided that we should break up.

When Michael came back to the flat that final time, to pick up the last of his things, it was very sad. He was so magnanimous, so gentle even at the end, giving me things, letting me keep things. When he left, I cried and cried, not because I wanted him back, but because I knew it was the end of an era. Looking back, I know that my relationship with Michael was never a failure. It was a comfortable period, a warm and good relationship. It was certainly exactly what I needed at the time.

I did sleep with Joe in the end, though our relationship only lasted a very short time. I think I just wanted him too much, was too passionate and he couldn't handle it.

Now I'm married. We have an agreement to be monogamous; I wouldn't break that, and if my husband had an affair I would be totally cut to pieces. I see that as the difference between my relationship with my husband and my relationship with Michael – I love both of them, but in very different ways. My love for my husband is a lifetime of love, love plus commitment, whereas my love for Michael was love for a friend.

Clare's dynamic with Michael is clear from the start. Her need for emotional support is met by his need to give it. They begin their relationship when they talk intimately about something that in different ways is important to both of them; Clare's having had an abortion links in to Michael's wish to have a family life with her. They spiral upwards happily on a loop of mutual interdependence. For his part, he assumes they will have a future together; she doesn't want this and moves away from Michael every time he mentions it.

Eventually, either Michael has to learn the truth and leave, or Clare has to change her mind. For the moment, both are getting a great deal from the relationship and the dynamic is stable.

Then, Clare makes a change. Because of a strongly emotional experience, she feels better about herself, and in the flush of self-love, spirals upwards with someone else who finds her equally attractive.

The man she chooses is involved elsewhere, and Clare is tempted to blame him for telling her he sees a future with her. But with great insight, she points out that when she is with him and his feelings interact with hers, then she is able to feel buoyant and optimistic. She allows him the same right to a positive, if unrealistic, viewpoint arising from their dynamic.

Then Clare discovers that Michael has had an affair. The interesting thing is not so much that she can bear it; her view of the relationship is such that we might expect her to be unthreatened. The crucial thing is that the affair has made a positive difference to their interaction, and Clare is clear-thinking enough to acknowledge this. Despite the fact that she is supposedly unconscious of it (though notice that, actually, she knows very well what is happening) she is affected by the difference in Michael's feelings and the new dynamic it creates. In having an affair, even though on a conscious level Michael thinks he is betraying Clare, he is actually stabilizing the relationship – by removing the emotional pressure.

Is Michael at fault? Within the dynamic they have, his affair in fact makes the situation with Clare happier. Therefore, although he broke his own set of rules and in that sense seems at fault, Clare herself admits to not wanting to 'expose it; things were actually better because he was having an affair'.

Equally, is Clare at fault? Clare is always straight with Michael; she consistently tells him that she does not see a future with him. Having met Joe and fallen in love, she does not want to give up either man. At no point, however, is Clare in any way consciously attempting to hurt Michael by her actions. On the contrary, her care in not making love with Joe before checking with Michael is proof of her responsibility to both of them.

In the event, however, the way the relationship has been set up makes it impossible for things to turn out the way Clare hopes. Michael still wants a long-term future with Clare and first tries to apply the sanction of blame to stop her looking elsewhere, then intensifies his involvement to create a more serious relationship. In both attempts he fails, and in fact Clare becomes more and more convinced that a serious relationship is not what she wants. The clearest statement of this she can make to Michael is to create the future he wants – a family life – and then to choose to spend it without him. This finally convinces him that she does not want to commit herself to him and, in the face of this, although Clare is happy to carry on, Michael himself has to withdraw from the relationship. Her action has at last communicated to him what all the words in the world could not do; he has at last heard clearly what her real beliefs are, and therefore it is impossible for the partnership to continue. Together they have brought it to an end.

Even though she is sad when Michael leaves, and even though her relationship with Joe never develops, Clare is ultimately able to step back, see the situation as it really was, and feel content with herself and with what has happened.

Rose

Rose is a work contact. Over lunch one day we started to explore other projects we are both involved in, and the book got mentioned. Rose began to talk, with wonderful candour, while I took notes over the salad.

Officially the 'other woman', Rose realized from the start that her relationship with Oliver was not a mere fling. But because he was married, they agreed to part. Imagine Rose's surprise when, a few weeks later, she received a phone call from Oliver's wife.

I was working in the same office as Oliver. It certainly wasn't love at first sight; he was sexually attractive, tall, slim and good-looking, but then a lot of men round the office were. There was nothing special between us.

One evening a whole group of us ended up in the pub after work and we two started talking. He came home with me, and it developed from there.

I never really wanted it to be serious. I had a thing about not getting involved with married men and I didn't want anything long term; I'd just finished living with someone myself. But we did get more and more involved, he more than me, I know; he was very jealous and very keen to be with me.

I never really felt like the 'other woman'. I thought too much of myself to ever think like that. I met Oliver's wife, Deborah, once, very early on before she knew about our affair, at a dreadful office party where Oliver and I were doing all the usual things like sneaking off round the corner to dance together. I remember feeling quite sorry for Deborah because, although she was much prettier than I am, she was small and dumpy and she was a 'wife'. I liked her, and in other circumstances we might even have been friends, but even though she was Oliver's partner, there was no way I wanted to be her.

Certainly I was attracted to Oliver because of his personality, and because he was very good at his job. As we worked together, I got to see him in action a great deal, and I had enormous respect for his professionalism. I don't know why he wanted me rather than her. I wasn't the office sex symbol, or God's gift to men. I was bright, lively, good at my job. She was a very home-based sort of person, but they had been together for a while, they had two young children, they had a good sex life. I still have no idea why he wanted me.

In the end, Oliver told his wife – again, I have no idea why. She was very upset, of course. I was upset too, and thought all the sensible thoughts, and said I didn't want any of it and that we should split up. I remember that it was all very tearful, but I was quite determined that we should finish. I spent a horrible, miserable few weeks – and of course it was made worse by the fact that we were working together, separated only by the space of two desks!

During that time I realized that the relationship meant more to me than just sex. There was a shift in the way I saw the relationship, and I realized that it was important to me, and that I did love him.

Then something amazing happened. Deborah rang me up and said that she couldn't stand Oliver being so miserable and would I see him again. It just seemed to me that it was ridiculous, bizarre; I was being all self-sacrificing and noble and his wife was telling us to carry on. So my reaction was, 'Is this woman crazy? Does she know what she's doing? Well, if she does, anything to oblige . . .'

Oliver came round to my flat the next morning on the way to work, and the whole thing started again.

Our relationship developed. Oliver used to say, 'Trust me, it will all work out and we will be together' – but he had two young children, and we both felt it would be very difficult for him to leave. So we lived this strange life. It wasn't too bad during the week because people at work knew we were a couple; I don't know what they thought about it, nobody said anything very much, but they all knew that he was still going home at night. He used to leave his home in the Sussex countryside at the crack of dawn, and drive into London, let himself into my flat at six o'clock and make passionate love to me until it was time for us to leave for work at seven.

Eventually though, I realized that I couldn't organise my life not knowing when he was going to arrive and when he wasn't. I just felt that my life was totally out of control. I was losing touch with all my friends and I needed to know what was happening, how long things were going to be like this. I got quite stroppy, and demanded a change.

So Oliver managed to persuade Deborah to let him spend one night with her and one night with me. For a while then, we did one day on, one day off, and that was fine. I had a great sexual relationship with Oliver every other night. The rest of the time I could go home and be a complete pig, eat sardine sandwiches, shave my legs if I wanted to. It actually suited me very well.

That went on for quite a long time, but then my old biological time clock started clicking away. I did love Oliver, he was lots of things I had looked for, and I decided I wanted a baby.

We talked about it; at first I said that I could have a baby whether he was with me or not. I must have been mad, but that was what I said – the naivety of it still horrifies me. So I got pregnant, and then I had a miscarriage. That was very upsetting, because the night I started to miscarry was not one of 'my nights' and so I was totally on my own. I broke the rules, rang him at home and said, 'You've got to come, I'm bleeding.'

He came. I lost the baby that night or the following morning. It was very early in the pregnancy, but I still found it incredibly traumatic, and after that I was depressed for quite a while. The next time I got pregnant, it was an ectopic pregnancy; I ended up getting rushed into hospital over Christmas for an operation and I lost a tube. It was after that that Oliver decided that he was going to leave Deborah. He says that it made him realize where he wanted to be.

At first I wasn't sure that I wanted him to move in. Sometimes I felt a bit as if he was trying to balance the scales – he had lived with her and given her two children and so now he must live with me and give me two children. But in the end, we decided to go for it, he and Deborah talked it through, and he left her for good. The irony of it was that the day he moved in with me, I was sent off to a job in the Middle East which ended up taking a whole month. Some honeymoon! I don't think he's ever really forgiven me for that.

We're married now. We have two children, we've been together for over ten years, and it's a good partnership.

It is difficult, though, that, even now, Deborah won't speak to me, or see our children; she doesn't hate me, but she can't bear to see us. Oliver's mother blames me to the extent that she won't meet me, and up to last week I had never even had a conversation with her on the phone.

When it was all happening, I thought at the time that the most amazing thing was Deborah ringing me up. Who knows what would have happened if she hadn't rung me. She certainly didn't want Oliver to leave; she genuinely thought he was the best thing that had ever happened in her life, and still does think that, as far as I know. But in some ways she was just as responsible for what happened as we were.

I think somebody probably told her to give him his head and that it would all burn itself out; and she was so frightened of losing him that she thought that was the best way to keep him. She always put him first, did what he wanted; but Oliver isn't like that, and it didn't work with him. She gave him enough rope and so she hanged herself.

Conversely, if I found out that Oliver was having an affair, then I would go bananas. He would be out of that door so fast his feet would never touch the ground. Now we are married, every time I am tempted to hold back on what I feel, or to give in to him, I think, 'No, he could have had that if that had been what he wanted; so that can't be what he wants. He wants me to be straight and demanding and going for what I want.' So I do.

I don't really think in terms of blame. It isn't a useful emotion because it doesn't help anyone. We were all to blame, and nobody was to blame. You could say Oliver was to blame for chatting up single women. You could say I was to blame for taking a married man home. You could say Deborah was to blame for not making sure that Oliver came home on the dot of seven every night. You can sling blame around like horse manure and it doesn't smell any sweeter.

Rose and Oliver begin their relationship with an easily identifiable spiral. We have no idea of the day-to-day dynamic that makes their relationship work, but from the start, Rose's strong independence and Oliver's jealousy all tell of an interaction based on pulling away on Rose's part and moving towards on Oliver's.

The dynamic is satisfying in that they both get what they want from it. It is also evolving in that something must give; either Rose has to pull away completely, or Oliver has to commit

57

himself completely. In the end, Oliver tells his wife, and Rose, unable to bear the tension of the affair, insists that they part.

Then, a number of very interesting things happen. The change-point of the break causes Rose to re-evaluate her situation. She realizes that the relationship is more serious than she had thought – but, despite this, had Oliver's wife not been who she is, the relationship might still have ended there.

Deborah's dynamic with Oliver is one of giving him space, and of making him happy. So when he is distraught because of Rose, Deborah's role is not only to allow him to have an affair, but to encourage him to do so. She asks Rose to take him back, she agrees to a 'one night on, one night off' arrangement and she gives, gives, gives, all the way through to a divorce.

As Rose points out, Oliver does not respond to this kind of emotional reaction in the way Deborah wants. Her apparent acceptance throughout the affair actually drives him away. Though the fact may surprise us, he is far more at ease with the reaction he receives from Rose, who states her needs and is clear about her dislikes. When faced with a lover who goes for what she wants and a wife who gives until it hurts, Oliver chooses the former – because he is that type of person. He and Rose spend more and more time together, fall more deeply in love, have children, and eventually, inevitably, move in together and marry. It is then that Deborah's acquiescence flips over into overt blame.

Rose is right when she questions the idea of blame. Who is to blame for this situation? All three are inextricably involved. Should we blame Oliver for wanting Rose, or Rose for wanting Oliver? Should we blame Deborah for allowing him enough freedom to want to go? Deborah thought she was acting for the best – and certainly was doing the best she could, but, in the end, her action actually resulted in the direct opposite of what she seems to have wanted.

It is easy to think of blame when faced with 'adulterous husbands' or 'wives out to hurt'. A story like this shows that the concept of blame breaks down when we are faced with someone who obviously acts for the best, but equally obviously is inescapably involved in bringing about the outcome they feared most.

Rose's attitude is a realistic one. She blames neither Deborah nor herself. But, equally, neither does she compromise. She goes for what she wants, and makes it clear to Oliver what will happen if she doesn't get it. And whereas one might think that Deborah's tolerance will win the day – which with someone other than Oliver it might have – in fact Rose's tougher stance, her 'sanction', is more appropriate simply because, in the end, this is what Oliver is able to respond to more positively. Rose's way of interacting with him results in a stable marriage; her awareness of what works and her ability to feel good about herself and those around her, even when the going gets rough, ensure that her relationship with Oliver is a success.

Influences

4 Double meanings

When an affair starts, we feel the impact immediately. How we think, how we feel, how we spend each moment – all are different, and all are affected at the most basic level.

'I felt as if I was walking on air,' said one interviewee. 'I have never hurt so much in my life,' said another. These effects, euphoric or painful, are what give the affair its meaning. They are the reality of a relationship, the actuality of the day-to-day effects an affair has on us.

But interview after interview also made it clear to me that the situation will in addition have a whole set of meanings for us other than the ones we see in day-to-day reality. The various aspects of the eternal triangle will also take on symbolic meanings and these symbolic meanings will crucially influence the way we think about the triangle. If we believe that adultery is immoral, then an affair will mean sin. If it is just a fling, then it will mean fun.

Equally, the symbolism that attaches itself to the eternal triangle can tell us how to judge the people in it. Should we condemn, envy or tolerate those involved – particularly if those people are ourselves? 'It runs in the family,' said one woman. 'Our women never do any housework and have lots of men. A long line of lazy women who love fucking!' Equally, the symbolism tells us how to feel about our primary relationships; does an affair mean the whole of the rest of your marriage was a sham, or does it mean that you have a stable and supportive partnership? 'I love my wife and want to stay with her,' said one man, 'but if I thought I would never sleep with anyone but her again in my whole life, I would feel my marriage was a trap.'

How does the meaning of what happens in a three-way relationship or how we interpret it affect its progress? Meaning dictates emotion, and so it affects the dynamic. If you enter an affair with a sense of excitement because for you it is a delightful risk, you will send round the triangle very different feelings than if you see an affair as a betrayal of your marriage vows. For Ruth, in Chapter 1, the symbolism of her physical relationship with Jon was virtually nil; she concentrated completely on the reality of the joy of sex. Conversely, the symbolism of emotional involvement prevented her from committing herself to Jon. For Deborah, in Chapter 3, who encouraged her husband to sleep with someone else, the symbolism of loving him enough to do so overcame the heartbreaking reality of his absence from family life – an absence which gradually drew him to transfer his affections to someone else.

How do we learn the symbolism of the eternal triangle? How does each of us build up in our minds a particular set of meanings that allows us to think of an affair as fun but our neighbour to consider it immoral? The dictates of our culture and our religion, our parents' views, the attitudes of our peers all tell us.

Particularly vital is our past history, our own earlier experiences. If we (or those close to us) have only had delightful liaisons, we will eagerly seek out others. Once we have suffered by being involved in a triangle, we will react more warily next time. This explains why the pattern of affairs for people in different age groups is always subtly different. 'Two-timing' in one's teens can mean a light prelude to 'the real thing'; in one's forties, it is more likely to be a distraction from, or a sought-after alternative to, one's primary relationship. For men and women too, because they are of different genders, brought up with different understandings of the world, the symbolism of affairs may well differ. Equally, there can be cultural differences; several interviewees spoke of seeing polygamy as admissible because it was acceptable in their country of origin.

It may be that our experience of sharing love is not directly sexual, but it nevertheless influences our attitude to sexual multiplicity. Many of my inteviewees related their beliefs about this back to early memories of their parents and the feelings they had about being excluded from parental friendship or being asked to side with one parent against the other. Such experiences prime us to place very particular symbolism on sexual triangles we meet in adult life.

What happens if the two sets of meanings – the actuality of having an affair, and the symbolism of it – differ for us? If you strongly disapprove of, but still get drawn towards three-way love, because the reality of it is irresistible, then you may feel mixed guilt, desire and resentment. All these feelings will complicate interactions with your partner or lover. Conversely, you may believe deeply in open marriage, but when presented with the reality, find yourself unable to cope with the jealousy it stirs in you. Attempting to hold together beliefs about the eternal triangle in the face of contradictory day-to-day reality can be very distressing.

One example of symbolism and reality clashing is the current concern with AIDS. I had expected to find interviewees worried about the effect of sexually transmitted diseases on their relationships – and some were. But a surprising number, particularly if they themselves had previously been monogamous for many years, felt that because taking a lover was a unique event for them, so special and so romantic, then the realities of safe sex (and contraception) could be ignored.

Equally, the symbolism and reality of the eternal triangle may change with events. If, like Clare in Chapter 3, you think that affairs are a bad thing, but then find that the fact that your spouse is having one has altered your relationship for the better, you may well feel confused, and this confusion will affect your interaction. If, like Tamar, later in this chapter, you live contentedly with an unfaithful husband for years and then suddenly find he is leaving you for his mistress, you may well feel that the world has fallen apart.

One classic problem that was highlighted during my interviews was this: when partners and lovers see very different meanings in what is happening to them, the dynamic can quickly spiral into conflict. 'Your sleeping with someone else means you don't love me,' says one. 'Don't be silly, it just means I get more sex/more attention/have a friend to take to the theatre,' says the other. The first attributes negative symbolic meanings to affairs, which bring them deep distress. The other has totally neutral symbolism, and simply wants a liaison for the positive effect it has on his or her day-to-day life. The resulting emotions inevitably lead to conflict.

Triangles that work almost always depend on the people involved attributing meanings to affairs that are complementary, if not identical. If everyone in a situation has complementary beliefs about an affair and the reality of their day-to-day lives reflects those beliefs, then what is happening will be acceptable to them. If everyone in the triangle believes it is just a fling – and acts accordingly – then the chances are that the affair will be a relatively painless one. However, if one thinks it is a fling, another hopes for commitment and the third sees it as a disaster, then the emotions this creates will inevitably move the dynamic to a painful conclusion.

Tamar

I visited Tamar at her house – she was totally triumphant because she had just signed a contract for it and was due to move to a new house in the following few weeks. A dark, handsome woman, she made me coffee and then sat, elbows on table, looking me in the eye whenever she talked.

For Tamar, the symbolism of the eternal triangle was never an issue, though she lived with it for many years. When at last things changed, however, they did so very dramatically.

I think my case is unusual because Alexander was never faithful to me. It was something I knew and accepted from the time we were married, and it didn't actually bother me. As long as I felt in control, I could handle things.

When I first met him, twenty-six years ago, we were both nineteen. I was working for a publisher and he was a salesman. From the beginning, no one else had the same appeal for me; I felt we were really on the same wavelength, and I wanted to be with him all the time. We met at a youth club and at first we went out with large crowds. He had someone else even then, a girl I'm still quite friendly with, in fact. It didn't worry me – it was more of a game than anything else. It all blew over, we settled down and got married.

We went out for four years before we finally got married. Neither of us had lived away from home until then, so we enjoyed it immensely. It was a great freedom to be young and married, with no real responsibilities except to each other. The children came along and, although it wasn't my choice at the time to have a family, they weren't a problem, mainly, I think, because Alexander played a large part in their babyhood. He was always there when I needed him – that time between five and seven in the evening is horrendous when children are little, and he was always there for that!

He had affairs right from the start. I don't know how many he had. I would get odd phone calls and work out that something fishy was going on; he'd come in late sometimes. He worked in the evenings, which made it easier for him not to let me know what was happening. We had one or two ups and downs with a couple of girls who were getting terribly involved with him, and we worked it out. On one occasion a particular affair was unsettling him, and in the end I just sat him down and told him he had to choose between the other woman and me; he accepted that and didn't see her any more.

I actually don't know what he got from having affairs; he said he couldn't help himself. He likes to think of himself as having a very positive, strong personality, but I think emotionally he's not very strong at all. I don't think he ever tried not to have affairs, because he just isn't very aware of himself, he isn't able to look inside himself at all.

It didn't actually bother me – I don't know why. He was coming home, wasn't any different with me or the children, our sex life was fine; I don't remember being aware of any problems. And I felt in control – not of him, but of myself. I don't think you can restrict another person, anyway; I accepted the marriage knowing that he was as he was, so I had no right to say, after a few years, 'Oh, you can't do that.' I liked him as he was, and his having affairs was part of the package. I knew from the first that he was never going to be faithful, and I didn't expect him to be. But I did expect him to stay married. It was a good marriage. We were friends, he was a terrific father, we were very alike in our sense of humour, we liked doing the same social things. I liked the couple we made.

I had one or two one-night stands myself, though nothing I would ever call an affair – by that I mean that I was never involved. I was in control of my emotions the whole time. I remember on one occasion helping a very close friend of ours get over his vasectomy operation! He hadn't been able to make love to his wife; we were alone in a car together one night, and I did my 'social services' bit! I told Alexander, and he didn't mind. I think it enhanced things – it does as long as your partner isn't going to be upset, and Alexander certainly wasn't.

When he began the affair that ended our marriage, I wasn't aware that the relationship had started – I think that's what upset me more than anything. I was aware, about a year before he left, that all was not well; he stopped talking to me, or at least stopped talking to me about anything that really mattered. He was ratty too, but he has a pretty awful temper anyway, so I suppose I just thought it was getting worse. There was no sexual problem, no problem other than that we'd stopped talking. These things happen so gradually that I suppose I didn't notice. Maybe I was just slow.

I know that around that time, I went back to work. I didn't want to go back to publishing, so I started working in a department store – and ended up in charge of the hat department! I really enjoyed it, but in some ways I think it hastened the end. Perhaps it's funny to say this about somebody who has walked out on you, but Alexander has a very over-developed sense of responsibility. I think he felt that if I could go out to work, I didn't need him so much.

I found out in the end that it had been going on for several years. Looking back, he might even have been the cause of her divorce, and I never knew! I only actually realized what was happening a few months before he left. We were at a Ladies Night and while we were dancing, I suddenly saw him glaring at a woman who was dancing with someone else. She's the sort of person who clings, vine-like, to whoever she's dancing with – and Alexander couldn't take that. He just glared at her, and then I knew.

I didn't do anything, just said, 'Stop staring, it's rude.' I was used to it, you see. He always goes for small, blonde girls, extrovert, well-made up, flash, with tight skirts, six-inch heels and rhinestones. I didn't think it was anything new.

A while later, he went away to a conference for a week. At the end of the week, I got a phone call from him to say he needed some time to himself and that he was going away for a while. I asked him where he was going, and he said he'd rented a flat. I think I just accepted that he needed time on his own, so I didn't even ask for the phone number. I didn't tell anyone what was happening, because, for the first time, I just didn't feel in control of what was going on. For the first time, I realized that there was somebody who had a stronger hold over him than I had. It was a very painful realization.

After about a week, he rang me and said, 'I'm making a mess of this. Can I come back?' So of course I said he could. When he came back we talked a lot. He said that he was in love, a blinding flash that had just hit him. I don't believe in that, not at forty years of age. I don't believe he ever tried to stop himself.

He stayed until December, then he felt he needed to leave again. Then I had to start telling people, start telling the children. It was very difficult. After about three months, I started getting phone calls in which he said he was missing me, missing the children, and then in March he said, 'I know what I want now. Can I come home?' I said 'Yes,' again, though I'm really not sure why.

He stayed for three months, which were absolutely terrible. He was obviously under extreme stress himself, and apart from when he very first came back, just wouldn't talk about it. And he told me that he couldn't make love to me, because I didn't turn him on any more. It is much harder to lie in bed at night next to someone you want to make love to you when they won't, than to be without them completely.

Then he went for good. I came home one day and found him packing, and realized that it was the end. He left that night and never came back.

At first, after he left, I wanted to know where he was and what he was doing. I had my spies out with reports coming in, but I've got past that stage now.

Whose fault was it? I blame her a lot; maybe she came into our social group looking for a new husband. I just wish it hadn't been mine. But I don't know for sure – I have no idea what was going on between them, what pressure she was putting on him.

Alexander always said, 'It's my fault. You've done nothing wrong. I have no criticism of you whatsoever. I can't help myself.' I probably agree with that. I think it is his fault. I'm loyal and if I've taken something on, then it's my responsibility and I will see it through to the end. But then again, one thing I have learned is not to judge. Some people would say it was outrageous of me to marry a man who had affairs and to accept that.

I did fight for him, particularly in the time he came back home for three months. I tried to be more interesting, more attractive, tried to arrange things that he would enjoy. It didn't work. But I don't think he went lightly; it took a lot of heart-searching for him to go. Maybe he felt that what we had wasn't enough.

I still see Alexander, give him a cup of coffee from time to time. I don't regret our marriage; I wouldn't have married anyone else.

But I still feel that if I met her in the street, I would take a punch at her.

From the start, Tamar accepts that her husband will have affairs; they have no negative symbolism for her. The things that really matter are that the everyday reality of life with him is good and that she is 'in control'.

Their dynamic settles into a stable and seemingly very happy pattern. He has an affair, she accepts it, he keeps the reality of family life stable by being there at the times she needs him. In return she supports him in his affairs. It is true to say that Tamar genuinely isn't upset. She and Alexander have an emotionally reciprocal relationship; she senses his commitment, he senses her acceptance of him.

There are one or two occasions when the dynamic begins to tip. Tamar, with insight, sees it as 'other girls getting involved'. When the emotion gets too high and feelings begin to impinge on family life, then she puts her foot down. And Alexander accepts this, for he, too, wants stability, and his emotions join with hers in stabilizing the relationship when it begins to rock.

Tamar is totally unthreatened by Alexander's 'infidelity' because her early experiences with him showed her that it would be all right; she would win. Anyway, it is part of the package – one symbolism for her of Alexander's affairs is that she is married to a sexually attractive man. It seems as if they will go for ever. As Tamar says, 'I did expect him to stay married.'

Except that it doesn't happen like that. A long-term affair turns serious, and we will never know quite why. Perhaps the early dynamic which so involved looking after the children was no longer taking effect. Perhaps, as she says, her increasing freedom altered their emotional relationship and made it easier for him to get involved elsewhere. Whatever the process, the result is that Alexander suddenly announces that he is having second thoughts about the marriage.

Everything changes. Not only does the reality of life with Alexander alter – he is no longer there, he no longer communicates with her, they stop sleeping together – but also the symbolism of affairs changes for Tamar. She is no longer in control. 'There was somebody who had a stronger hold over him than I had ... and it was a painful realization.' Nothing that Tamar can do works – because the time for doing is long past. Now the emphasis is all on feeling, and the feelings have changed.

Tamar's relationship changes in both its reality and its symbolism. Instead of a husband who hides his affairs and is there when she needs him, she has a husband who leaves her. Instead of a husband whose bond is to her, she has one who owes his loyalty elsewhere. The interesting thing about Tamar's story is that for so many years she is genuinely happy with the symbolism of affairs, because the reality of what is happening totally meets her needs. When it all changes, so does her happiness.

Charles

Charles came to visit me. It was a very hot day and we sat in easy-chairs with the windows open and the smell of honeysuckle wafting in from the garden. It was a slow, careful interview, full of pauses and consideration.

For Charles, the symbolism of his wife's affairs is minimal. He sees them as totally unthreatening to an otherwise happy marriage. For a while, his wife agrees, but slowly her view changes.

I'm really not sure that my experience is relevant to this book, because although my wife and I were in an eternal triangle, I felt that that had nothing to do with our splitting up.

Let me set the scene. When Mary and I married, I certainly felt that I was committing myself to her for the rest of my life. It was important to us to get married, and we never considered living together. But I certainly didn't feel that I would be getting everything I wanted from her.

Our marriage seemed at first, and for a long time, to be very good. We had a lot of fun together, and we built something together. We worked for the same company, but we both had outside interests.

The one thing that was never quite right was our sex life. It may have had something to do with the fact that, when I was younger, I went through a long period of feeling that sex wasn't possible at all for me; it was something that other people did. Mary must have had some equivalent, and it led to a lack of permission, an absence of sheer feeling. I felt very early on in our marriage that sex wasn't good and that created a barrier, for both of us. We quickly got into a pattern where we only made love when we were going to bed anyway, and then in the same position.

For Mary I think sex with me was a duty. She lay back and thought of England. She would, for example, be looking at her watch while we were making love to check whether it was time for her to make a particular phone call. Eventually, I became reconciled to the idea that if I wanted good sex, I was going to have to get it outside our relationship, although I didn't actually have an affair until after we split up.

A few years into our marriage, Mary met someone else at work. She started an affair with him, although she did say that she only had sex with him because he wanted it. I really felt that that was a part of her life that didn't involve me. I didn't feel there was any threat, in any way. We once went out together, the three of us; my thought is that she wanted proof that I was happy about the fact that she was sleeping with him. I felt a bit uncomfortable about that, because I didn't feel the need to meet him and didn't get on with him particularly. But he didn't feel like a threat.

I think the thing for her was that she was not getting much out of sex with me, and with him it was much more spontaneous and enjoyable. She liked the change. I certainly felt that it wasn't up to me to restrict what she was doing and I didn't feel it was actually a problem. It did mean that I also got permission to meet other people and go out with them, although we never slept together.

There was anger, but it was all about not being told what was happening. She didn't actually tell me that her affair had been going on until a while after it started. She hadn't trusted me enough. It wasn't the act but the secrecy that angered me.

That relationship finished when Mary's lover moved away. I don't think that anything else could have happened. She certainly didn't give me the impression that she saw him as a long-term possibility, and she probably gave the same message to him. Equally, he seemed to me to be very unassertive, apologetic and anxious to please. So I don't think he would have gone very strongly for what he wanted, even had he wanted her.

Our relationship carried on and it was still good. We had fun together and enjoyed each other's company. We ate together a lot, enjoyed each other's cooking, went out to the pub and drank good beer, went on some lovely holidays. We didn't make love very often, and we did argue and never quite dealt with that, but, nevertheless, it was very much worth carrying on.

There was something else happening too. In hindsight, I think I was still deeply in love with someone else, someone I had known for a long time before, though I had no awareness of that at the time. My emotions were really somewhere else, with somebody else. This came to a head when Tara, the person concerned, came down to see us and stayed overnight. There was never any question of anything happening between us, because she was entering a religious order. When she came to stay, however, I wanted to see her alone. I thought I had discussed with Mary whether Tara and I would go out somewhere for a chat, but then I realized that Mary thought that she was coming too and I allowed her to see how disappointed I was. I think that could be one of the reasons why Mary lost interest.

Again, a little later, I fell in love with Alison, someone I worked with. We trusted each other and became very close. It was entirely a working relationship until things happened in the office and we both felt she had been very badly treated. She was moved away from my section and I realized that I wanted to carry on seeing her; I also realized that I had fallen in love with her. I hadn't been conscious of that before.

When I actually told Alison how I felt about her, she couldn't cope with it. Our working relationship was important to her, but she couldn't handle my other feelings. She said she didn't even want us to be friends any more. In some ways, the strength of my emotions pushed her away.

That was a really bad period for me. I was having a bad time at work, and I had lost Alison's friendship. I wasn't sleeping sometimes, and once or twice I went into rages, not violent towards Mary, but uncontrollably angry. I feel quite guilty about that. Mary supported me very well through those times, gave me a lot of support. She put up with a lot.

We had about a year then when we didn't make love at all, although after that things got better; however, we still didn't sleep together very much. That was a barrier between us, but it certainly didn't mean that our relationship was at an end. We were still enjoying each other's company. I feel that by then sex didn't actually mean anything to Mary. I certainly wanted sex, and was explicitly looking to have an affair. There had been a couple of times when I'd shown interest in other women, but they'd said, 'No, not if you're married.'

Mary was getting more and more unhappy. Once, she talked to her family about it, and they suddenly began talking to me about it. That made me angry. I didn't like the fact that they talked to me as if I was causing the problem, when in fact Mary hadn't told me at that point that there *was* a problem! I felt blamed, and annoyed that she had not trusted me enough to tell me how she felt.

Then she started seeing Andrew. I'd met him already, at a party; I'd quite liked him, although I don't like his appearance. There is something about him that is quite unattractive. I knew they were seeing a lot of each other, but at first I didn't know they were sleeping together.

But I still didn't feel I was affected by whom she spent her time with. I am very clear that I felt I wasn't losing anything by it.

Then one day, Mary came to me again to say that she thought we ought to separate. I have a clear image of us both sitting on the chesterfield in our living room, not touching, just talking.

She said she had come to believe that she would never want me sexually, and yet she knew I wanted sex. As my wife, living with me, she didn't feel she could say no continuously, but she couldn't be happy with saying yes. We both thought of marriage as a commitment, and she didn't feel she could say she had a commitment to me when she was unhappy having a sexual relationship with me.

Personally, I felt I had made a commitment. We still enjoyed each other's company, and I would have stuck with it – but I was at least glad that Mary had talked it through with me this time rather than just telling her family. What mattered to me was waiting for a few weeks to check that she still felt the same. I wanted to make sure it was not just a thought of hers, and I wanted to be sure I'd done what I could to help us work through it. I would have liked to go to Marriage Guidance to try to work it through, and I did suggest that, but she said no. She felt she had made her mind up and it was time to get out.

So after a few weeks, once I was clear that Mary had made her decision, I was actually happy for us to split up. Mary got herself a flat, and I helped her move.

I have to admit that I don't feel there was a connection between the fact that Mary went out with Andrew and then we split up. That's supported by the fact that when she first left, she went into accommodation on her own, then bought a flat on her own; it was only when she became pregnant by Andrew that she decided to move in with him.

I get on with Mary really well still, though I don't feel I want a major connection with her. We are separated, but not divorced – not so much because we still need to be married, more because we don't feel married so we don't need to be divorced. We still work in the same company, so I see her quite a lot there, but not very often outside. Andrew now feels

that he isn't comfortable for the three of us to meet, so Mary
and I only see each other when he isn't there.

I still regard our marriage as mostly a success.

For Charles, affairs have no negative symbolism in his marriage.
He has no special symbolism around fidelity, and he enters his
relationship with Mary specifically aware that he will probably
not get everything he needs from her.

The reality of their relationship is very positive. They are good
friends and, at first, even the dwindling sex life is not a problem.
Even if it is, they both agree that it is acceptable to take lovers
outside the relationship without threat.

It is this that allows them, at the beginning, to ride the disheart-
ening reality of a less than perfect sex life in favour of the good
times they have together. Charles certainly does not feel that his
marriage or his manhood are under threat, even when Mary
takes a lover.

The dynamic is stable. Had Charles seen Mary's affair as a
problem, either because it reduced the quality of her interaction
with him, or because it seemed somehow 'wrong', then he would
have demanded a change. The relationship would very quickly
have destabilized one way or the other, Mary choosing to remain
faithful or to leave the relationship. As it is, they create a satisfactory dynamic of mutual acceptance which remains stable for
a number of years. Mary is not interested in finding a new
relationship, her first lover does not push the matter, and so the
affair resolves itself without a hiccup.

However, the partnership between Charles and Mary is not
totally stable. It is moving slowly and surely in the direction of a
change-point. The first movement comes when Charles shows
his affection for Tara. This does affect Mary; her emotions start
to shift. And when that situation repeats itself with Alison, we
suspect that Mary's emotions once more shift.

Slowly and inexorably, Mary's idea of what is happening
changes. She finds that the symbolism of not sleeping with
Charles is not acceptable to her. It is not a problem to him, in the
context of the rewarding reality of their relationship – but it is to

her. Whatever particular emotional dynamic causes this, whatever movements forward and back, whatever responses between them, the end result is that, for Mary, the end arrives.

The important thing about Charles's story is that he is in no way lying when he says that Mary's affairs are not important to him. He, like many others, genuinely sees the symbolism of affairs as totally subordinate to the reality of his relationship, a reality which, despite an unsatisfactory sexual relationship, is very much worth while. In the end, he is right. It is neither the symbolism nor the reality of the eternal triangle that separates him from Mary, it is the symbolism of their diminishing sexual relationship, highlighted by her affair.

Isobel

I travelled by train to meet Isobel on a hot sunny day in August; as I walked out into the station forecourt, she was leaning back on her estate car bonnet, a slim blonde figure in chopped-off jeans and T-shirt.

We went back to her house, collapsed on her sofa and drank herbal tea. She had hay fever, and sneezes and giggles punctuated the whole interview. Later, she commented that whenever she talks deeply, her 'respiratory bits' act up to show her that something is being disturbed.

Isobel was divorced several years ago, but remained in an eternal triangle with her husband for several years after the divorce.

I married the guy who had the fun of taking my virginity. I really did want to marry him, fell in love with him. The first time I met him, when I was seventeen, I went home thinking 'This is the man I'm going to marry'. Neil is six years older than me, very tall, very fit, very muscular – and always very solid and mature; he was born middle-aged. Initially, that was what I liked about him, and eventually that was what drove me round the twist. From him I got stability, reassurance, a father figure for a few years while I grew up.

For him, I was a prize. I was intelligent, articulate, attractive, had an interesting job. I was capable and I could cope with everything. We had the whole set-up after about ten years – lovely house in the country, estate car, dogs, green wellies.

But after we were married, Neil left me alone a lot because of his job, which was flying. Also he wasn't interested in the same things as I was; I was a sociable person, out every night, I did a lot of amateur dramatics. There was a group of young people who went round with each other; I was one of the few who were married, but the young men were always available to take me out. Neil didn't mind that. He wanted me to enjoy myself, so I did. He seemed to think I needed space.

He didn't like to discuss feelings, but occasionally we would talk about what would happen if either of us found someone else. He didn't want to talk about my having an affair, though I did need reassurance that he wouldn't leave me. Looking back on it, I think he would have been prepared to put up with my relationships as long as we'd stayed married. As long as it wasn't public, I could do as I liked.

The first time I had an important affair, it was with Adam, a friend of Neil's. He was very unlike Neil physically, fat and dark, but he was such a friend, such a lovely person to talk to. He was sensitive, comforting, and we were very close indeed.

Adam wanted us to set up home together. In the end he even tried to push me to make a decision, to choose between Neil and himself. But I knew it wouldn't have worked on a day-to-day basis. I wanted to stay with Neil, where I felt secure. So one day, when we were visiting Neil's parents for a family celebration, I sort of 'engineered' a confession to Neil. That brought things to a head and made us end the affair. Adam was very upset – and so was Neil. He felt that he had trusted both Adam and I, his friend and his wife, and we had betrayed him.

Neil didn't at the time seem to know about my previous casual relationships; later he said he had known, but they hadn't meant anything. It was my affair with Adam that hurt. I think sleeping with other people was all right with him; it was sleeping with Adam that was wrong, was a betrayal of trust.

After that I had my first child and stayed faithful for a year or two. Then I was at a New Year's party, on my own, and met Gerry. We danced, and I liked it. I said, 'I don't want to go home alone tonight. Will you come home with me?' He refused, saying that he had to go home because his wife was at home; I thought how boring that was.

But it didn't put me off, so I arranged to see him and we began an affair that lasted a long time. He was a wonderful lover; he enjoyed talking with me, sharing things. He loved my unconventionality and my enthusiasm, my spontaneity.

It got very serious; I met his parents, and at one point we were actually going to live together. He was abroad at the time, and he told his wife what was happening and then came back to me. I met him at the airport; I remember I had injured both my ankles at the time and could hardly drive! When I met him, he told me that things had changed. His wife had had a breakdown and was mentally ill. Gerry himself was very sensitive and I know that he couldn't just walk away from her, couldn't ignore her. She was like a sick animal. So he stayed.

I was very angry with her; I knew I myself wouldn't have fallen apart over things like that. Now, I wouldn't do anything to hurt another woman because I've had so much support from them, so looking back, I feel quite sad about how I felt and behaved. I regarded other women as competition – I was brought up to believe that.

I didn't tell Neil about the affair with Gerry; it didn't seem to have anything to do with him because he was away so much. Later, much later, he told me that he knew all the time. He didn't choose to challenge it or act on it because he didn't want us to split up.

After Gerry, I settled down to try to sort out my marriage. I knew that I was still in love with Neil, and so I worked on it. I did have a brief affair or two, but Neil and I were getting on well together, going out, entertaining people, bringing up our family. Neil was quite happy, wanted me to enjoy myself as long as I didn't interfere with his life.

Then my old job as an editor became vacant, so I started work again, and working there too was Jonathan. At first, we didn't have an affair; I'd decided to have nothing more to do with married men! Strangely, his wife thought we were sleeping together, and Jonathan actually asked me to go and see her to reassure her. I did so, reluctantly. She was a mousy little thing, very insecure.

In the end, I did have an affair with him because I was absolutely bowled over by him. It became a total obsession. It was a very different relationship from any of the previous ones I'd had. We were so similar; there were so many things I didn't seem to have to explain to him. He seemed to know, about me, about himself, about our insecurities. The sex was very good, full of communication and understanding.

Also, Jonathan seemed to offer me a future. Life with Neil was fine; I had three kids, lots of money, plenty of good things – but I was totally appalled at the thought of going on like this for another fifteen years. Jonathan and I kept planning to do all sorts of things – start a business, open an art gallery. I might add that now, ten years on, we have done none of these things. We don't even own a typewriter between us, and that makes me angry.

This time, Neil brought it all to a head. He had suspected something, though he had not challenged me – but then things had changed for him. He had changed jobs away from the area we lived in, and I refused to move with him because I didn't want to lose my support system or my social life. He hunted through all my things and found some incriminating letters; which he lodged with a bank.

Then he gave me an ultimatum. He told Jonathan and me to decide what we wanted to do – either I was to move with him or we would divorce. I didn't want to move with him, but I didn't want to divorce either. I was sick of the lifestyle and we no longer got on, but I was afraid of being alone, afraid of managing the finances. But a short while later, Neil lost his job, and when the financial support I needed was no longer there, I was quite happy to divorce. And so we did.

We continued to sleep together though, irregularly, every couple of months. We saw a lot of each other, because of the children, and I visited him when he was working abroad. We always did have a good sex life, so it seemed natural to carry on sleeping together. In fact I needed both him and Jonathan. I needed Neil's security and stability; I needed him to be the children's father; I needed the chemistry, the good sex. With Jonathan I needed the talking, the understanding. I still needed both of them, and certainly the triangle of my sleeping with both of them continued for about six years.

I went through a change with Neil about eight months ago. He was being very loving, saying how much he still loved me, how much he wanted another child with me. I thought this was too much, and I realized that I didn't actually want a relationship with him any more, so now I only speak to him through the children and leave them to work out their relationship with him directly. Up to a few months ago, however, I still felt emotionally dependent on Neil. Then I had a two-night stand with a guy who had exactly the same body, exactly the same mind as Neil had twenty years ago. By sleeping with that guy, by showing myself exactly what it was I was attracted to, I exorcized the attraction to Neil.

Jonathan and I are still together, though we don't live together. Eventually he left his wife, and we tried moving in together. It lasted six weeks and was a disaster. So, although we're still going out, he's becoming less and less involved with what I am doing, and it's becoming less and less possible to talk to him. We have our no-go areas, we avoid rows, but I don't tell him what's in my heart. Although now he is 'trying very hard', as I put it, I don't see us as having a long-term future.

I don't think I'm naturally monogamous; I always seem to need two men in my life. I would really like to have lots of men in my life so that I could indulge in all the things I like doing and share them. It's unrealistic to expect one person to fulfil every aspect of your life and I certainly wouldn't tell my children that it was necessary to have only one relationship.

So it will be interesting to see, in a few years, whether I am involved in yet another triangle. Will I go on as I have in the past, or will I be able to supply for myself whatever it is I need from men?

Isobel and her husband seem to have an ideal match. She is left alone a great deal, because of Neil's job, so the marriage could have become lonely. Instead, as Neil does not seem to mind, Isobel goes out a great deal and has the opportunity to have affairs. Which she does. It becomes clear very soon that Neil attaches no negative symbolism to her taking lovers as long as it does not become public.

At first, Isobel is after the fun and the excitement. Then she has a more involved affair. When her lover threatens to become too serious, she tips the dynamic over by 'engineering a confession' and thus restoring the status quo.

This first real affair does affect Neil emotionally, principally because he feels that for Isobel to sleep with one of his friends is wrong; the symbolism of this is not acceptable to him, even though the general symbolism of Isobel's taking a lover is.

When Isobel's next serious affair occurs, we can see the dynamic inching its way slowly towards ultimate break-up. This time, there are plans to leave Neil. In the end, the relationship breaks up after Isobel's lover stays with his wife – pulled by a dynamic of guilt and emotional pressure that keeps his marriage stable.

Again, Neil knows about the affair, even though Isobel hides it from him. Still the reality of their marriage is sufficient for him to accept what is happening without challenge.

Isobel's next affair is even more serious. She falls for someone who offers her many of the things which Neil does not, and suddenly this affair is vital. In particular, the future with Jonathan is much brighter than the potential future with Neil.

This time, Neil does challenge what is happening. Amazingly, however, it is not because this affair is any more serious than the others, but because the day-to-day good things of his marriage are threatened; Isobel is refusing to go with him when he moves. He 'discovers' her letters and gives her an ultimatum.

Isobel at first hesitates, but she does not want a divorce because the day-to-day impact of a break-up on her life would be difficult to handle. When the lifestyle she had with Neil is no longer forthcoming, she is happy to divorce him. It is fascinating that for neither her nor Neil is the symbolism of affairs a crucial element in their break-up; they could have carried on quite happily had their own day-to-day lifestyles not been threatened. Hence, unlike many couples who feel betrayed by their partners, they have no reason not to continue wanting a relationship with each other once they are divorced.

Now, Isobel is breaking free of both of the men in her life. She is positive about affairs, seeing them as fulfilling her various needs, and judges whether an eternal triangle works very much in terms of the direct effect it has on her life. She is beginning to see, however, that the eternal triangle may represent for her an inability to cope on her own — and so she feels positive about breaking free of it.

5 Wanting and getting

Agendas – what we want, and what we aim for – are crucial in eternal triangles. Because they are about wanting, and hence about the emotions of wanting, they will affect us and through us affect others around us. Our wanting emotions – desperation, need, attraction, lust – will tilt the dynamic this way and that in an attempt to reach their goal.

Agendas may not just be about wanting to have something – or someone. We may want *not* to have. Others may be about moving towards: seeking love, demanding sex, longing for cuddles. Many are about moving away: wanting not to be left, avoiding rejection, fearing an unfulfilled life. So the passion dance between the three becomes even more complex; as everyone moves towards what they want and away from what they don't want they create ripples that move the others too.

Agendas will often differ according to age, gender or cultural group. We usually aim for the needs and wants we have been led to expect over the years. If a woman has, over twenty years of girlhood and thirty years of marriage, been led to regard an undisturbed family life as her chief agenda, she will do anything to achieve this and to avoid disturbance of it – even accepting the otherwise unacceptable fact of her husband's 'adultery'.

I found in my interviews that people's agendas were often about the way they wanted an affair to affect their primary relationship. This resulted in a range of kinds of affairs from 'light and lively', which have no real impact on the primary relationship, through to ones which essentially aimed at swapping one long-term monogamous 'marriage' for another. Often the agenda for the 'wandering' partner was to lever themselves into leaving their partnership completely, even though the affair that triggered the split then became irrelevant and was ended.

Several interviewees accused their partners of being 'incapable of commitment' and suspected that they kept having affairs to stop any one primary relationship becoming too intimate and important.

Sometimes, conversely, the main aim of an affair was to stabilize the primary relationship by filling the gaps this relationship did not satisfy – the affair actually supported the main partnership, and, if the affair ended, that partnership suffered. Wanting an affair for this reason was not, in fact, always an agenda only for the 'erring' partner. Often a spouse, seeing a partner flourishing when he or she had affairs, would encourage them to continue because of the positive effect on their partnership.

Explanations of affairs which try to categorize them into the 'Casanova pattern', the 'short fling' and the 'start-a-second-family affair' type usually use agendas as the basis of their categorization. It is not the whole story, for relationships are far more complex than that; knowing people's agendas, however, is a useful focus in understanding the conscious motivation behind an affair. Equally, knowing what you and your co-participants in a triangle really want is a useful tool. If your partner wants new experiences, but also values commitment, then he or she will probably choose to stay, despite the occasional fling – and knowing that may both reassure you and enable you to plan for trouble if agendas suddenly change.

The best kind of eternal triangle is when everyone is getting what they want all the time. Very occasionally, these situations do happen. If A wants an affair for variety and a partnership for security, and B wants A to stay in their mutual relationship but doesn't mind if they enjoy themselves outside, and C wants excitement but not commitment – then everyone will get what they want. This is how long-term triangles survive, the stereotypical situation where the wife is happy, the mistress is happy, and the husband commutes happily between the two.

The worst kind of triangle is where agendas are unconscious, mixed, changing, or conflicting. Then, since needs are not met, and feelings rise in order to *make* things happen, everyone's emotions destabilize – so rows and break ups or reconciliations follow. It is always the case that the strongest feeling affects the dynamic the most – and where agendas are vital, the emotions can be very strong indeed.

If you know what you want, but in reality it is only what you *think* you want, then you have an unconscious agenda. Because you don't recognize it, you will find yourself intending to act one way and actually acting differently. You will agree to something, and then mysteriously find yourself disliking or sabotaging it. Also, your real emotions will communicate themselves to others, creating spirals that are even more distressing because you have no idea why they are happening. 'I said I was happy to keep the affair secret,' said one woman, 'but I obviously wasn't; I found myself continuously leaving evidence around and then was shattered when his wife found out!'

If you want more than one thing, then you have a mixed agenda. This is particularly likely for the partner who wants love from more than one person; in Chapter 2, for example, James wanted to make love with both Bindu and Jeanette. For a while he had both, but for most of us, the situation is rarely so simple; often we cannot have everything, but must choose.

Equally, eternal triangles, with their complex dynamic, almost always force mixed agendas into becoming a hierarchy, an agenda tree where what we want is rated in descending order of importance. The relationship evolves, some agendas become less possible and less attractive, others become more possible and more attractive, and the conclusion becomes inevitable. Even if you want to remain married *and* keep your lover, things will change – one way or another. For James, being committed to Jeanette became more vital than continuing to make love with Bindu.

Equally, even if everyone in a triangle wants the same thing, they will rarely want the same things in the same order. For Charles, in Chapter 4, it was more important to have an enjoyable friendship with his wife than for her to be faithful. And as long as that was true for her, the relationship was stable. When it changed, and, for her, the issue of their sex life became all important, the dynamic tilted and things had to alter.

Hierarchies sometimes work well in a triangle. If a lover's

highest agenda is to have fun, while a partner's is to have a family life, then an 'uninvolved liaison' will probably result. If the balance tips, however, and the lover suddenly also places family life at the top of their agenda tree, emotions will switch dramatically and the effect on the situation will be just as dramatic.

For agendas do change. As situations change, some things become less important and others more – which explains why so many partnerships wobble at just the point when the agendas they were set up to meet, are met. When the children grow up, when the business flourishes, when one or the other partner grows through the insecurity that drew them into the relationship in the first place, then suddenly and inexplicably, an affair begins – or ends.

Finally, and most obviously, eternal triangles are notorious for conflicting agendas. Where one person wants the freedom of a liaison and the other the stability of monogamy, or where one person wants to stay married and the other wants him (or her) to leave that marriage, then real conflict is inevitable.

I found that the 'happy triangles' I came across were characterized by complementary agendas – and this usually meant that agendas were discussed openly. In this way, partners and lovers, knowing each other's agendas, were more able to meet them. Often they saw such discussion, and the ensuing negotiation or agreement to meet agendas, as a 'contract' they had between them, and were clear about what such a contract involved. Couples might discuss, for example, what having an affair meant to them, who was allowed to have an affair, under what circumstances, whether the 'lover' was allowed in the marital bed. Lovers might develop a contract covering the need for secrecy, time spent together, the possibility of ever forming a partnership. 'It's fine as long as it's safe sex and I don't know about it,' commented one interviewee. 'She made it clear from the start that her marriage was sacrosanct,' said another.

Such discussion may seem cold-blooded, but in fact we all do have agreements about such things, whether they are talked about or not. Such rules exist in all relationships, but they are often unwritten; for example, when it is assumed by both a husband and wife that an affair will totally destroy their marriage, it is often never stated. It is when the understanding of the unwritten contract differs from one person to another that there will be problems, as many a lover who has assumed that 'she will leave her husband one day, because she really wants to be with me . . .' has found out to his cost. When someone else fails to meet your agendas because they don't agree with them, then that is distressing, but you can at least negotiate, compromise or leave. When they fail to meet your agendas because they don't agree with them – and you thought they did – then that can be the end of the world.

Robert

Robert visited me one afternoon, and we sat and talked. He is currently living with a partner he has now been with for over five years. For Robert, the agenda issue is a mixed one. He and his partner are committed to each other, but their agendas around the eternal triangle are very different. Robert has found ways for himself to reconcile his situation.

I'm currently involved in a long-term relationship with my partner, Pru. The deal we have is that our relationship is monogamous, and she's made it very clear that she wouldn't be able to cope with any other kind of set-up, that she herself wouldn't look for any sexual relationships outside our own, and that she would be devastated if I were to get involved elsewhere. It isn't anything moral, it's that she could not cope with the jealousy and the pain.

I know she's happy with the fact that I have strong friendships, and strong sources of support. She likes the fact that she doesn't have to fill my entire life and meet my every need. But she does draw a very clear line around actual sexual relationships and it is a fairly literal line which is about fucking. For me, I have to say, the actual act of penetrative sex isn't a betrayal, so we differ there. And although we have an agreement, an informal contract about relationships, had I been making that agreement all on my own, it certainly wouldn't have included anything about not fucking. That isn't what it is about for me. I would like a contract I made to have a sense in which the core relationship was central, but which didn't necessarily insist on faithfulness at the level of detailed behaviours.

About three years ago, I started a relationship with Jessica. I met her through professional interests and we ran a particular discussion group in which we were both very influential. It was clear to both of us from the beginning that we were attracted, but for a long while it was not clear what we intended to do about it. The attraction was there though: strong, immediate, arousing, sexual. There was also a tremendous sense of fascination with each other's worlds. There was one particular evening when we spent some time together, shared a meal and talked, and I had the most immense sense of openness, excitement and connection.

That was in November. The next significant thing happened just after Christmas. I came back from the holiday very angry at Pru over a family issue, an area where we had a lot of differences at that time. I realized then that I was beginning to be very dissatisfied with the whole thing of living together, more and more convinced that I was limiting myself in this relationship. All of a sudden I began to think about the first stages of leaving. We rearranged our furniture a bit, I started sleeping in another room, I began to look at possibilities for living somewhere else.

It seems as if all this was about my relationship with Pru, but in fact a great deal of it was about my friendship with Jessica. There was certainly a strong contrast between the two women when it came to possibilities. I could see two totally different ways of being me and I could project them on to Jessica and on to Pru. Certainly, at the time, I was definitely feeling that I would vote for what Jessica stood for, the other way of being me.

Things went backwards and forwards from January to April. I was openly discussing with Pru the possibility of leaving, but at the same time it wasn't clear what was happening.

Then I started sleeping with Jessica. It happened like this. I went to the professional discussion group, which was held at her house, and I 'missed' the last tube home. I put the word in inverted commas because I found out subsequently that the tubes ran later than I thought they did – but at the time I really believed that I'd missed the train. So I had to stay overnight. The first time this happened, we didn't make love together, though we did have sexual contact. On the second occasion, we did. We fucked, and we had an orgasm together.

I told Pru about it. I was pleased to be able to do that, because I don't enjoy hiding things, and I enjoyed being open. She didn't like it at all, but it was acceptable in some way, because we both believed I was leaving. It certainly wasn't a question of 'I've slept with somebody else and I'm leaving you', more 'I'm leaving you and I've just slept with somebody else'. We both knew that there were other things contributing to our parting, so although Pru didn't approve, it wasn't a breach of our contract. Our contract was suspended, not abolished, but certainly in abeyance, because we thought we were splitting up.

I don't think I ever thought Jessica was a likely candidate for me to set up home with. It was in my mind, and at one level it was what I was aiming for, though I knew it wasn't possible. She has exiled herself from domesticity, in some ways she has always been on the run from long-term domesticated relationships, so such a thought was very dangerous for her. And in that sense, when I was preparing to leave, Jessica couldn't give me the support I needed in order to make it work. At the time I was planning to leave, for example, she was planning two extended trips out of the country, and that really made me stop and think.

We'd noticed in the past that we have a dynamic of my

moving towards and her moving away, although there was also a dynamic of my backing off if I thought she was becoming too available, and hence less exotic, because that wasn't what I wanted from her. We talked about it afterwards and she wondered what would have happened had she been able to support me. Maybe things would have been very different.

As it was, this was what happened. Towards the end of April, I fixed up alternative accommodation. I found what I would call a 'sympathetic' household, which was comfortable, affordable and in an area of London where I had lots of friends. I'd sorted out all my possessions, told my ex-wife and the children I was moving and even gave out the new address. I was due to move house on the Friday.

On the Tuesday I woke up immobilized. I had pulled a muscle in my back and couldn't walk. I was bed-ridden for a week, which of course meant I couldn't move – in both senses of the word.

I spent that week thinking and considering my options. Pru was great, very supportive in both an emotional and a physical sense. I rang friends and talked it through with them. I gradually came round to thinking that maybe I shouldn't move – and as soon as I had made that decision, I recovered very quickly, and that was significant.

I took my illness as a message that I was right to stay, and that my thought of leaving had been a mistake. I have a habit of doing that – I create options in my mind which are actually false options, but which I find reasons to carry on with even though they are harmful or threatening. Then as I work towards them, my intuition and my body combine to correct my error by sabotaging my false move, usually through a strong physical manifestation such as an illness.

Of course, once I'd decided to stay, the contract with Pru around monogamy was in force again. Jessica had decided to go abroad for a while, so I was able to tell Pru that she wasn't around, or expected to be around. The question still remained what I would do when Jessica returned, and I told Pru that I wanted to be friends with Jessica, but that we wouldn't be sexually involved.

I followed through with that, but I was deceitful about the timing. Pru assumed that I was not sexually involved with Jessica after April, but in fact we were sexual with each other for several months afterwards. After that, things were getting better with Pru, and I wanted them to keep getting better; so, however difficult it might be for me, I knew that I wanted to end the affair. If I was still sexually involved with Jessica, Pru would realize it on a subconscious level and know that I was not fully there for her.

I told Jessica before Christmas that I wasn't going to be sexual with her any more. My timing wasn't good. She had just come back from yet another trip abroad, she was exhausted and really needed support. She accepted what I was saying, but she heard me say that I didn't want to be sexual with her, which angered her; I did still want to, but I had decided not to because of Pru. I also think that Jessica wanted more of me than she was getting, more time and more energy.

We worked through it very well, I have to say. The openness and clear communication that formed part of my original attraction to Jessica enabled us to talk it through and resolve it very clearly and effectively, so the friendship soon settled to a different sort of level. The wonderful thing is that the exoticism is still around, this special quality of contact.

I suppose, in the end, I'm in a bit of a double bind. I have made a contract with Pru, and if I fall in love with someone else, such as Jessica, then I am in breach of that contract. If I don't, then I betray my true value system which is about giving myself possibilities, and to me that is a more fundamental betrayal.

What I think Pru is signalling to me by her attitude is that in some way she is happy for me to fall in love, but that she does want to avoid being hurt, which is possible if she doesn't know what is happening.

We seem to have a situation where our value systems don't fit and our agendas are not the same. They are now comparable or negotiable in every other aspect of our lives, but sexuality is the one area where they are not. It would be worse, I think, to have a partner with whom I apparently had everything in common, but whose agenda was very different underneath. What I like about being with Pru is that we are pretty clear that we don't see eye to eye – and we work within that.

Robert and his partner have very different agendas as to how a relationship should be. They are both clear that freedom and a rich social life are important, but for Pru sexual monogamy is on the agenda, and for Robert it isn't.

He is very clear about the emotions that lie behind these: Pru's fear, his need for possibilities and fulfilment. He includes sex in these possibilities; a large part of his aim in wanting affairs seems to be access to another person's world, to exoticism, to add to what he is getting from his relationship. Where these include sex, however, then there is a total conflict with Pru's agenda.

This conflict must, at some point, lead to Robert stepping outside his agreement and taking action – or, as he says, betraying himself at a fundamental level. He says himself that he is not fully congruent about the agreement he has made, but it is not until he and Pru are on the point of splitting up, and the 'contract' between them is essentially in abeyance, that he takes the risk of having an affair and stepping outside the contract.

The dynamic between Pru and Robert has pushed them further and further apart; they have already moved more or less to the point of separating, and it is this which gives Robert permission to sleep with Jessica. Equally, as he points out, his dynamic with Jessica is pulling him towards her and away from

Pru. These two sets of movement together seem irresistible.

Just as he is about to leave, several things happen. Jessica has already pulled back by arranging some trips abroad, and it is possible that this emotional communication has made Robert pull back too. Alternatively, he may be pulling back already, needing to keep intact the element of magic in his relationship with her.

Despite this, Robert seems ready to leave. His conscious agenda is all about a new life, away from Pru and towards alternative possibilities. It seems as if the main agenda of his affair is to break up his relationship with Pru. But this is not the whole story.

Robert's unconscious agenda is very different from his conscious one. The benefits of staying are obvious, but Robert has ignored them. When he continues to ignore them, some part of him acts; he wakes up one morning immobilized and has to reconsider his options.

It may seem far-fetched to say that Robert's unconscious agenda made him ill. He certainly believes this, however, and it is his illness that makes him realize this unconscious agenda. He is encouraged to do this when, in response to his illness, and to his rethinking the situation, Pru is very supportive. Robert becomes even more aware that some part of him wants to stay, and once he decides to, his back problem clears up.

He finds it difficult, once the contract is in force again, to justify continuing to sleep with Jessica, but he does so, gradually winding down the relationship so that, eventually, it is platonic.

In some ways, Robert's situation continues to contain mixed agendas. He wants to follow his own personal fulfilment, but at the same time to remain loyal to Pru and not hurt her. His solution is not to discuss his other sexual attractions with her until and unless they have a common frame of reference for discussing them.

He comments, accurately, that one of the problems of his relationship with Pru is that they have different agendas about affairs. As he also says, they are clear about that, and that is a better option than conscious similarity, hiding unconscious disagreement.

Mya

I met Mya on neutral ground, a Women's Centre in the student area of the town where she lives. She is in her thirties, dark and pretty, with black curly hair framing her heart-shaped face. We sat in one of the counselling rooms, on hard, uncomfortable chairs, drinking coffee from the Women's Centre café, and talking through her story.

For Mya and her partner, affairs are a way of life. They meet and fall in love largely because they know that their ideas about relationships are very similar, and that they can accept and support the eternal triangles (and squares) that they each enjoy.

But then something changes; because their situation alters, their idea of what is right alters, and immediately there is conflict of the deepest kind.

I met my husband, Aaron, because we moved in the same circles. At first, I really disliked him, but then one night we spent some time together in a pub and I found he was quite nice to be with.

From the beginning, he was seeing other people and so was I. I was quite happy with that, and could totally accept it. But we were really keen on each other, making declarations of love – and I have to admit that I felt it was the best thing that had ever happened to me. I really felt for the first time that I could be totally honest, really free, and do what I always wanted to do. From the start, we talked through everything and laid down guidelines for our relationship.

Aaron's reason for taking other lovers has always been that the culture he comes from is non-monogamous; there, they have more than one wife. For me, it is more personal; I just don't think I am naturally monogamous. I do have a lot of men friends whom I don't sleep with, but I also like to have more than one lover. I feel that it is very difficult to get from one person everything I need and I like to get different things from different people. Also, I frequently think the grass is greener on the other side. I'm often curious about what someone is like in bed, and so want to make love with them to find out. I like variety in love-making, different ways of doing it, lots of different lovers. I've always been like that, and it is rarely to do with something being wrong with a relationship, although if I feel that my partner doesn't care for me then I will take a lover as a reaction to that.

For a while, my relationship with Aaron was wonderful. But then, about eight months after we'd started going out together everything changed.

It happened like this. I'd been to Paris with a girlfriend, and when I came back I brought lots of French wine back with me. It was really hot, and Aaron and I went out on the verandah drinking and getting very passionate. Live Aid was on all night, a background of music, and I felt wonderful, sexual and sensual. I keep my contraceptive cap in the bathroom upstairs, and when we went from the verandah to the bedroom next door, I just didn't bother to go up and get it. It was too far away. I remember Aaron saying, 'Oh, it's the wrong time of the month for you to conceive. Don't worry.' But I did conceive.

In hindsight, I know that both of us wanted a child. At the time, Aaron only had one child, and had split up with that child's mother. So he didn't often see his baby and was feeling bereft and abandoned. I had had a miscarriage eighteen months before, so I really wanted a child too. I never thought of having an abortion. I just couldn't.

When I told Aaron I was pregnant, everything changed. Bit by bit he started moving in to my place. At first he said that he just wanted to store things in the loft, but then I gradually realized that he was moving more and more of his stuff in, and himself along with it. I didn't want that. I felt out of control and got very angry.

Then we started talking about getting married. I'm very aware that there were the reasons we talked about and the ones we didn't talk about, didn't even admit to ourselves. We said that we wanted to confirm our trust and understanding, we said that it wouldn't change anything, we said that we wanted to care for our child better, we said that marriage would make it easier for him to stay in this country. I think now that our real reasons were very different. He was worried that he might lose his child if we weren't married, and I thought that being married would stop all the hassle I was getting from my family and friends.

From the start, our expectations changed. He started expecting me to be at home a lot and look after our child. He stopped going out with me. He really expected me to stop seeing other people; but he didn't stop – he was having an affair right from the start of our marriage.

I knew about his affair. He often went to see a friend called Rachel. He said their relationship was platonic, and that he slept on her settee when he stayed the night. Yet she kept ringing the flat asking to speak to him, and although I put up with that for a while, eventually I simply asked her straight out, 'You keep ringing up and asking for Aaron. Are you his lover?' and she said, 'Well, yes, I am.' I realized that he hadn't told her about being married or about having a child. She knew nothing.

It started to matter to me then that he was having an affair. Previously it hadn't, but then it started to matter. I no longer felt that things were balanced: I was having fewer lovers than he was, and he was lying to me. I got very angry and resentful.

Then Aaron found out that I had a lover. I'd told him I was going away for the weekend, but instead I left our baby with a sitter near where we lived and spent the time with my lover. I went to a night club with him and, quite by chance, Aaron walked in and saw us there. I really hadn't expected him to be there as he never went to that night club, but I just looked up and there he was. It was the first time that I'd had an affair and not told him.

Aaron didn't come over and drag me away; in fact I went

back to my lover's house, stayed there the weekend and came back on the Monday as I'd intended to. Then there was a big row; Aaron kept asking who on earth the guy was, and also what I'd done with our baby.

In return, I called his bluff, and told him I knew about Rachel. We rowed and rowed. He said that he was going to end his affair and that I should end mine. He kept saying that having affairs wasn't healthy and that we ought to act like responsible adults. He insisted that we each ring our lovers there and then and finish the relationships. In fact I was quite happy to do that, as my lover was about to leave the country anyway, though I didn't tell Aaron that.

Rachel was totally devastated, though. She was shattered by his finishing their affair, but more shattered by the fact that he'd lied to her. She contacted me and we met up in a pub to talk; I spent quite a while with her, listening to her and consoling her. I felt really sorry for her – she was a kindred spirit – but I found it all very disturbing.

That put me off open relationships for a long time, and we had a period of stability. I felt so bad about it all, and particularly about Rachel, that I thought 'Well, if Aaron doesn't have affairs, then I won't either.'

It hasn't happened like that though. Aaron got into another affair, and so did I. It seems we have a pattern: we don't have affairs, then we do; when I can't take it any more I split us up, then he comes rushing back; then we have some stability for a year or so. Then the whole pattern starts again.

Recently, Aaron has started again. So I am left with a choice. Do I cut off from him, do I leave and form another relationship with someone else, do I start having affairs again myself?

It was very difficult to analyse our relationship. We know each other, we are still married, people know us as a couple. I have his child. We still have a strong passion, and very deep, strong feelings for each other. That's very important to me. If

I were to split up from him, I would need someone with whom I could have that strong emotion – and I know he would need that too.

Yet we both need to have other partners, and that is now a problem. It is also difficult with our little girl growing up; she notices a lot, and if she finds me in bed with a lover, then she gets upset. So I am aware that Aaron has a lot more freedom than I have to take lovers, and that makes me very angry. He has a lot of girlfriends, and although he says his relationships are platonic, I don't believe it. And I don't like him having partners: if a woman rings up for him, I now say, 'Who the fuck are you?'

I always tell my partners I'm married but separated, and they seem to accept that. I have been with partners who try to persuade me to divorce him. Some of them offer me safety with them, but I don't actually want that. If they ask me to choose, I always say no. I don't want to choose. I still feel a lot for Aaron, and I don't want to be owned again.

There's an extra twist to the tale now. I think I may be pregnant, and I'm sure it is by Aaron. I will have to decide very soon whether to go through with it.

If I do decide to have an abortion, I won't tell him.

Mya and her husband begin their relationship with agendas that are clear. Each of them prefers to have more than one partner. The symbolism of that for each of them is that it means they are free. The reality is that affairs give them pleasure.

Neither of them then has any problems combining this with a committed relationship, and at first it seems to work very well. Certainly Mya feels that in her relationship with Aaron she is meeting her agenda; she wants the pleasure of having affairs, the security and affection of a stable relationship, the ability to be honest. She and Aaron talk through their agreement and are both clear about what they want. Their agendas are conscious and complementary. Hence they are able to have a stable dynamic based on mutual emotional support; where one has an affair, the other accepts and gives permission for it, and vice versa.

Then Mya falls pregnant. She is clear-sighted enough to admit that although it was an unconscious agenda for them, it was nevertheless something they both wanted.

In the wake of the pregnancy, however, everything changes. The symbolism of their relationship changes dramatically for Aaron and, as a result, his agenda changes. From being about freedom and support, they suddenly shift to being about commitment and family life.

Aaron's agenda shifts too much for Mya to follow him. Although they are both still aiming for sexual freedom, he now also has an agenda involving Mya being faithful, her caring for their child, her providing a stable family life for him.

This immediately creates an unstable dynamic. Although before, an affair on either part would lead to emotional support, now it leads to fear, anger, jealousy. They now feel they have to hide their affairs, which in turn leads to more negative emotion. The whole relationship rocks.

A number of emotional spirals, which Mya describes with great insight, happen over and over. No affairs, affairs, increasing rows, reconciliations, no affairs – it seems very painful indeed. But both of them keep doing it, and have done so consistently for several years. Their agenda is not about ending their relationship, but about having the freedom to have affairs and still keep their relationship stable.

Mya's emotions, and hence her agenda, switch somewhat when she meets Rachel. This emotional communication with Aaron's lover does affect Mya, and for a while she remains faithful as a result.

But slowly the dynamic tilts over again, they each become more and more inclined to have affairs, and Mya tells us it has just recently changed once again into a triangle.

The key issue is always their agendas. If they were still single and without a child they could, in theory, have remained in a stable open relationship, because what they wanted was complementary. Instead, they now have conflicting agendas and the result is of course a dynamic of conflict.

Daniel and Victoria

I spoke to Daniel first, a work colleague who then contacted
Victoria and got permission for me to phone her. When I did so,
we realized that we had met previously, and the phone call was
punctuated with laughter as we swapped mutual memories.

The two interviews together form a moving account of how
unconscious, changing agendas can lead to unexplained and
misunderstood dynamics.

Daniel

I met Victoria first at a residential weekend. We got on well,
but there was nothing really sexual except that, at one point, I
was rubbing her back and I think both of us were aware that
she was enjoying it. Nothing really happened until we met
about six months later, at another course, and she and her
woman friend had nowhere to stay.

I invited them to stay at our place and when we got there I
offered Victoria a choice: there were two double beds, and she
could sleep with her friend or with me. She chose to sleep with
me, and when we got into bed together, we both decided that
we wanted it to go further.

The relationship was very good for me. She would come and
spend occasional weekends at my place; we would stay in bed
a lot, make love a lot, stay up all night talking. We went out
very rarely, just once for a meal, I think, and once or twice for
walks.

I try never to define any relationship as central, and so I am
usually not monogamous and feel uneasy with the concept. It
didn't worry me that Victoria was married. I knew her
husband was ill, and that she felt betrayed by his illness
because she believed he had brought it on himself. He was
quite deliberately killing himself; knowing that he was dying,
he continued to smoke something like sixty cigarettes a day,

and so in a sense he was choosing to be an invalid, and had therefore withdrawn from a relationship with her. She felt that to survive at all she had to get her pleasure somewhere else, and that was fine by me. I thought of my flat as somewhere she could come to escape and enjoy herself, a place for topping-up sanity.

About a year after we had started seeing each other, Victoria's husband died. She rang me shortly after it had happened and we spent a long time talking about it on the phone. I thought it would make a change in our relationship, but I expected the change to be positive. I thought I could now spend more time with her at her house, more freely. I'm sure she was looking forward to that too.

But it didn't happen like that. From the second or third time I went up to see her it started going wrong. I am a critical person, and though I was trying hard not to be critical with Victoria, it did creep out, more in her house than mine. After twenty years of living with her husband and being criticized by him, she was hypersensitive and easily hurt by this. Yet in a perverse kind of way, she was bringing out the critical side of me. She was used to it, she needed it, she created it.

Things never really worked, and after about six months we had a fairly melodramatic row and I walked out. She'd been very spiteful and vindictive and I felt I had to get out of the house or I might have hit her, so I went. I never felt happy about that, though, and I wanted to tie up loose ends.

So about six months later I phoned Victoria from work, late one night, and we had a long, long conversation. I seem to remember that at the end of it she said something like, 'It was really nice talking to you again. I'd really like to see you.' So we met up and started seeing each other again.

That lasted for a while, but then she met someone else, another guy who fell for her very heavily. At first she didn't want to know about him, but after he'd bombarded her with bunches of roses for a couple of weeks, she changed her mind!

It all ended very abruptly when I went to spend a weekend with her. A row developed out of nowhere and just as I started to challenge what she was doing, the other guy arrived early to see her. I said he should sit and wait for fifteen minutes until we'd finished, and she flared up about that and said I was jealous. She told me to get out of her life — so I did.

In hindsight, I think that when her husband was alive, Victoria needed an escape, a sort of courtship. But once he died and she was free to have a more long-term relationship, a stable one, she looked to me for that and it just wasn't possible. That led to our splitting up.

Yet there was enough there for us to get back together — and we did until someone came along who could give her the long-term relationship she wanted. Then, although she said she wanted to stay friends with me, it felt as if she deliberately precipitated a situation where we weren't going to stay friends so there was no danger to her other relationship.

I think I've recognized most of this in hindsight; I was too close to it all at the time to realize what was happening.

Victoria

I first met Daniel several years ago. We split up after a row and haven't really had good contact since. I have no idea why we split up — it just happened. When he rang me to ask me to do this interview he suggested we should meet up, but I'm not sure.

We first got to know each other at a residential weekend. There are no clear memories, we just got on really well. There was only one moment I remember. We were standing talking in the kitchen; we'd just been very open with each other and Daniel had thanked me for being honest. I thought to myself, 'Yes, I really could get close to you.'

It was not until the next residential weekend that we got

together. He simply asked me to spend the night with him, and I said yes.

He was a superb lover. He has a very good body. And he really takes the time and the trouble to find out what a person wants — well, he did with me, at any rate — willing to experiment and try things and really check out what is wanted. It was wonderful, and our affair started there.

I would go down to stay with him quite regularly, taking a few days or a weekend off. His room became a little world apart where we could escape to together. I could talk to him about anything and he would be really there for me. He would make me the centre of his attention — he has superb attention. He had energy and insight and intelligence, and he would really care for me. It was all great fun. We would spend lots of time in bed, give each other massages, eat meals together, go for walks, go for trips in the car. It was all very different from what I was doing at home.

My situation was this. I was married, but there was no real relationship with Colin, my husband. He was very ill, had been for ten years, knew he was dying and I knew it too. He was smoking himself to death, was dying of emphysema. I felt very angry towards him for that, and for what it had done to the family, my son and daughter.

You have to realize that all this was vital to me. It was a way of having my life, of giving me back my confidence in myself and my femininity. So although there was some guilt there, it was far more important to keep going for what I wanted, to have some purpose in life.

About eighteen months after we met, I went down to spend New Year with Daniel. We had a good time, and on New Year's Day I travelled back up North to my family. I had no idea of what was coming. When I arrived, my husband seemed a little better and had been cooking dinner. We ate the meal and then I went to watch *The Deer Hunter* on television. I thought I heard him call out, but he didn't call again so I didn't really worry. After a bit, I went through to see how he was and I could see right away that he was actually on the point of dying. I went towards him and he opened his mouth to say something, just looked at me and died.

I sat down and shook all over. And do you know, my main feeling was one of relief.

My relationship with Daniel was never the same after Colin died; I don't know why. Daniel came to see me, but it was never the same. He didn't really fit in, he didn't get on with my son. It just didn't feel right. It was just different.

I met someone else after a while. His wife died too; there are parallels in our personal histories and we had a purpose in each other's lives. Daniel didn't like my new partner, he thought he wasn't right for me because he wasn't into personal development.

In the end, Daniel and I split up. We started to argue, things got heavy, and he stormed out. We met a while ago and went for a long walk on the moors, but it still didn't work, we were still tense around each other.

While I've been telling my story, I've realized some things I didn't realize before. It really feels as if my relationship with Daniel fulfilled a purpose; it gave me something outside the problems of my marriage and helped me to survive. But then, when my husband died, I didn't need the relationship any more. The purpose was over, the need was no longer there.

I did once feel very good about Daniel. After my husband died, I felt differently about him, but I now think that was because the want was no longer there.

I wonder how Daniel feels about it. Maybe I will contact him and talk it through. If he feels the same, maybe we could start communicating again in an honest and open way. Perhaps we could.

The fascinating thing here is that these unconscious agendas only surface during the course of the interviews themselves. The effect of this, for Victoria at any rate, is dramatic; it totally transforms her view of what happened. She realizes that the argument she had with Daniel was not simply coincidence, but was a change-point in the dynamic which had been built in from the start.

Victoria's relationship with her husband had obviously destabilized long before her affair with Daniel started. She and Colin already had a dynamic based on negative emotions, and this pushed Victoria into seeking positive emotion elsewhere. She enters the relationship with Daniel as part of a conscious plan to have a life outside the prison of living with her invalid husband. Her agenda is clear; she wants confidence, femininity, sexuality, a purpose in life.

All these she can get from Daniel. He is sexual, attentive, caring. For him, she is a friendly and comfortable partner whose company he enjoys. They build a mutual loop of attraction that spirals upwards and upwards.

When Victoria's husband dies, her guilt is real. But what she does not realize is that she also has changed agendas. Now she no longer has a sick husband from whom she wants to get away. Her needs are very different, while Daniel's agenda remains the same. Now she no longer wants escape, but a longer-term relationship. Immediately Victoria's emotions alter, and the difference in her relationship with Daniel is at once noticeable. He resists her changed agenda, refusing to take her husband's place in the situation; his agenda is just the same – to enjoy her company.

It takes a while longer for the dynamic to destabilize totally; they split up, but come back together again. Eventually, however, the change-point occurs. When Victoria finds someone with whom she wants to have a stable and committed relationship, the dynamic between her and Daniel finally tilts over; they row and he leaves.

Victoria's change of agenda is totally unconscious, even up to the start of the interview, and Daniel also is 'too close' to the situation to recognize what is happening. Had they realized more clearly what was happening, Victoria could, as she now plans to do, have simply talked to Daniel openly, and the relationship might have resolved itself very differently. Maybe they will be able to do this now that they have understood more fully what was happening.

6 Mixed messages

Communication is the glue that binds relationships together – and in the eternal triangle, that most intimate of relationships, the communication between all the people involved is a crucial element determining what happens in every dynamic.

Who communicates, and with whom, in a three-way relationship? A simpler question to answer is: who does not communicate? Everyone has to communicate whether they like it or not, simply by virtue of being involved with each other. As I explained in Chapter 2, even if two of the people involved do not meet each other – even if they do not know of each other's existence – they send messages round the triangle by means of the one linking factor, their loved one.

What do people communicate? As I have said earlier, the words and actions by themselves are not important. If you have ever been told 'I love you' by someone who has stopped loving you, you will know only too well that words are meaningless when divorced from the emotion behind them. The feelings are the vital elements transmitted in the communication, the ones that most affect the people we are relating to, the ones that most move the dynamic on. The emotions we communicate are, quite simply, whichever ones we are feeling at the time. We cannot help this. Even if we are attempting to act differently, our feelings inform our interactions.

Understanding emotional communication, particularly in a situation as complex as a triangle, does not mean attempting to work out rules for human behaviour. To say, 'Never be angry with an erring spouse' (or 'Always be angry with an erring spouse') is missing the point. In certain circumstances, with some people, anger may work very well; with others, in certain situations, it will produce the opposite effect from the one you want.

True understanding of emotional communication means looking at what is happening between all three people and charting its progress, noticing how people respond to others in certain situations, and what effect this response has.

Because feelings are complex, we can never make a blanket prediction as to what effect they will have. Only when you understand someone very well can you know whether they will respond to a particular request with loving compliance or rigid refusal. Even when you do know this, you need to be aware that in different contexts, faced with different demands, their response will differ – and once a relationship is complicated by the addition of a third person, their response may be totally altered. A normally placid partner, made vulnerable by a threatened affair, may respond with sadness where once they would have been happy, or with compliance where once they would have complained.

Emotional communications within a dynamic are also capable of 'transformation'. I discovered as I talked to interviewees that it is rarely a question of one feeling being passed round the triangle, so that if husband feels grief-stricken, then so does wife and so does lover. As each emotion passes from one person to another, it will become transformed and passed on as some other, often totally different one. A husband's jealousy, received by the wife, can make her feel guilty; this transforms itself by the time she meets her lover into anger against the lover, against herself, against the situation.

Receiving this communication, the lover may become more concerned, more affectionate – and this communicates itself to the wife. By the time she meets her husband again this has been transformed into resentment that her spouse cannot be as considerate as her lover ... which in turn could well lead the husband to become even more jealous.

From my interviews, I identified three elements that influence just how the communication of emotion affects a dynamic. The first is intensity. As an emotion is communicated round the triangle, it is the intensity of that communication that pushes the situation to a change-point. Just one intense interaction may spiral a three-way relationship into a new pattern; a single, ecstatic meeting with a lover is sometimes enough to call into question a life-time commitment. The positivity of the feeling is unimportant when compared with the intensity. Angst is just as much of a driving force as lust; one traumatic row may end an affair for ever. Simply, the stronger the emotion, the more it tips the dynamic over, and the more likely that dynamic is to move quickly into a new configuration.

Vital, too, is whether the communication is given consciously or unconsciously. When we talk of unconscious communication we are not thinking of the Freudian realms of darkness but of the unconscious part of our minds that we are not normally aware of. If you know you want to sleep with your lover, but do not know that you also want intellectual stimulation from him, you may be unaware that it is you who are starting deep and meaningful conversations at bedtime – and you will then wonder why the dynamic is going in a different direction to the one you expected!

Equally important is whether the communication is received consciously or unconsciously. Conscious communication is easy to receive because we can react to it directly and challenge it immediately. If you are unaware of what your lover is communicating to you, then you may be unaware of why you are feeling as you are, and therefore be unable to understand what is happening to your dynamic. In all senses, unconscious communication is crucial, simply because you cannot control it; unconscious messages slip through our social defence lines, affecting us deeply. If you have ever been in a situation of feeling unaccountably uneasy in your lover's company, then you will know just how disruptive that can be. Because you don't know what is causing the problem, because you cannot discuss it or resolve it, because you may even be unaware there is a problem – things are difficult. Once the reasons are out in the open, then you can act.

A final vital element concerns how many emotions we are trying to communicate. If you are unsure of your aims and beliefs, what you really want, or what you are trying to avoid, then you will be mixed (incongruent) in your feelings. Your communication will vary, first expressing one emotion, then another, perhaps moving towards and then moving away. In an eternal triangle, where people are often unsure of what they feel, incongruent communication can be a way of life. Each person may give mixed messages on their own behalf, and two together may give very different accounts of what is happening. As a result, spirals that tip first one way then another can become part of one's everyday life.

They can also be part of one's everyday misery. Incongruence is acutely uncomfortable for human beings. Children can become schizophrenic when faced with constant incongruence; adults can become violent when the mixed messages get too strong. So, whether it is you, your spouse or your lover who feels conflicting emotions, the effect on the triangle will be the same, causing distress and trauma. Many of my interviewees reported breathing a sigh of relief when 'he decided to go – not because I wanted him out, but simply because at last I didn't have to cope with the flip-flops.'

Marguerite

Marguerite contacted me through a listings magazine, and we talked on the phone. She is a bubbly Scottish lady who talked happily about her current relationship and how successful it is. Her story is one of looking for sexual fulfilment and rarely finding it – until she met the man who is to become her second husband, and with whom she had a wonderful sex life. Then, following an operation, Marguerite's husband became impotent, and this inevitably changed things.

I married the first chap I ever went to bed with, and he was a virgin as well. I never enjoyed sex with him, and even when I took a lover, very early on in our marriage, I found that painful too. I had a number of affairs, but I always felt a freak; the girls at work kept saying how great sex was, but I thought I was frigid. I was convinced that I was never going to enjoy making love.

Eventually, when my husband and I were on the point of splitting up, I ended up having dinner with one of the doctors where I worked. Over the meal, I'd had a few drinks, and I said to him, 'Well, you can forget about anything else because I'm frigid.' He said perhaps we could work something out – and we did. He was the best thing I'd ever had in bed, and after that I knew I wasn't frigid and that there was no way I could stay married to my husband. In the end, he left to work in Nigeria.

A month after he left, I started working in a new office. I quite fancied my boss James, who was divorced, too, and about the same age as me. I rather threw myself at him, phoned him up and suggested we meet for lunch, told him I'd split up from my husband and asked whether he fancied going out with me. He did.

James was very good in bed, and that was incredibly important to me, for obvious reasons. We had a very good time in bed for a long while, and he was the first person ever to bring me to orgasm. It happened like this; when I met him, I knew I'd never had an orgasm and didn't really know what one was. Then we went on holiday to the States and were sharing a room with another couple the whole time. We couldn't do anything really, but in the middle of the holiday it was my birthday, and I wanted to make love. We decided we'd make love in a way the other couple couldn't see; so he came into me from behind and touched me at the same time – and it happened. It was amazing, and totally unexpected.

Then, just before James and I got married, he hurt his back and we couldn't make love very often because it was painful for him. It made our honeymoon a bit odd, but we weathered that.

When we came back from honeymoon, a terrible thing happened. He was diagnosed as having a spinal tumour and was in hospital for six months, having all sorts of treatment. He had radiotherapy, spinal fusion, chemotherapy. He said later that if he had known what he was going to have to go through, he would have committed suicide. When he came out he was still in a lot of pain and very debilitated.

Also, he was impotent. At first I accepted that, for he had had a lot of pain and a lot of problems. We tried to make love once or twice, but it just didn't work. I had realized that if he half-woke in the night, then he had an erection, so there couldn't be anything physically wrong. I had thought that if it was physical, I could accept that; we would come to some sort of arrangement. But once I realized that it wasn't physical, I also realized that he could probably do something about it. So after three and a half years, when love-making was still a rarity, I could feel my sexuality stirring, and I broached the subject.

We were sitting up in bed one night, and I simply said, 'We have to talk. We haven't made love for a while. I think you have a problem.' His answer was 'I don't have a problem – I'm forty years of age. I just don't fancy it.' I suggested to him that it was probably a mental problem; at first he was shocked, but then he agreed to go to the doctor. But when the doctor suggested he go to a psychosexual clinic, he was livid. He is the sort of person who doesn't believe in mental problems, and he was appalled at the thought that his impotence might be all in his mind.

I remember that we booked into a hotel for a romantic weekend over St Valentine's Day; it was a total disaster. A few weeks later, I bought some sexy black underwear and dragged him up to bed; again nothing happened.

I had been faithful for three and a half years. I really wanted to be; I really wanted to be faithful to James, as I hadn't been to my first husband. I know that if either of my husbands had been unfaithful to me, I would have gone bananas, so I wanted to be faithful if I could.

In the end, I met someone at work who was the first person for four years that I had actually physically fancied. He was single, not good-looking, but slim and attractive and very nice. I had a kiss and a cuddle with him at the Christmas party, and then chased him for about two months, but he was quite moral and refused to do anything because I was married.

When we actually did get together, he was brilliant. He really showed me what I was missing. But he treated me badly, insulted me, told me that I was a scarlet woman. At first, I had thought we would be quite nice together; he was an accountant, very well off, we shared a lot of interests in common. But he thought so badly of me, wouldn't even introduce me to his family, that I knew early on that it wasn't going to go anywhere. We only spent a couple of nights together.

In the end, my husband and I split up. I wanted to have an affair, but felt I couldn't do that and still stay married, so we planned for a divorce. When I told my accountant, he was furious. He backed off immediately; he didn't want to be involved when the shit hit the fan. But he was just what I needed at the time, a sort of lever to give me a push to get out and get what I wanted. I didn't have very high self-esteem at that time, and I needed him to show me I was attractive by going out with me. When he did, I felt better about myself and was able to make the move.

I'm still friends with my husband, though it's four years now since we split up. He has secondary growths now from his tumour, though he keeps moderately well. It was only last year that we really talked properly about how we came to split up. By now, he's realized what really happened, and so have I.

He says that after he was ill, he felt that he married me under false pretences. He said if he'd been diagnosed before we got married, he probably wouldn't have gone ahead with the wedding. He was so guilty that he just couldn't get an erection; he's had girlfriends since we split up without any problem, but it was just that he felt guilty about me. He feels he ruined my life, though I tell him he hasn't.

For Marguerite, everything to do with sex is emotionally charged. With a history of fearing frigidity, of not being able to enjoy love-making, she places vital importance on a good sex life. Is it any wonder that she chooses to marry someone who is the best lover she has ever had? We learn little about their relationship out of bed; whatever dynamics they have between them, however, one thing is certain – her ecstasy and anxiety around sex must transmit themselves to her husband.

When he becomes ill, this triggers an emotional spiral between them. He cannot make love at first, and this, we learn with hindsight, makes him feel guilty; Marguerite probably responded in a number of ways, a mixture of support, disappointment, patience – and in some way this obviously spiralled James into yet more guilt and yet more impotence.

Why does he not simply state how guilty he feels? Why does he not communicate directly to Marguerite that he feels he has let her down? At the time, James is unaware of why he is doing what he is doing. For reasons of his own, he cannot admit his guilt; it is only later that he comes to realize that his impotence is not purely physical. So his communication is truly unconscious – he knows what is happening but, at the time, he has no idea what it means.

There is an added benefit to the particular method of communication he chooses. I have stated before how comparatively unimportant words are. James's communication of his guilt through his impotence is a much stronger statement than any verbal one – and it is one that Marguerite cannot ignore.

Supportive though Marguerite is, she does not continue to be sympathetic when James will not agree to take action about his impotence. Their dynamic then flips over; she is increasingly withdrawn in response to his impotence, and he becomes increasingly guilt-ridden that she is not getting the life he wants for her, so they spiral into a continuing lack of sex. It is to both their credit that they keep the relationship stable and use their affection for each other to hold back the slide; it is over three years before the spiral prompts Marguerite into having an affair.

This affair acts as a lever, proving to Marguerite that her marriage is at an end. The triangle lasts a very short time, but it is long enough to fulfil her agenda to disrupt her relationship with James completely and allow her to get out of what has now become a disappointing marriage. The affair is in many ways her communication to him that the marriage is over.

In some ways for Marguerite, the eternal triangle is a catalyst in the serious business of finding a new and more satisfying sexual partner. It is significant, and not unexpected, that because sex is so important for Marguerite, the emotional communications between her and James are centred around sex.

Spencer

Spencer rang me and we met in the centre of London. We had no idea where to go to talk, and travelled slightly aimlessly on the Tube until we emerged at Marble Arch. The interview that follows, conducted on the grassy roundabout facing Hyde Park, was one of the most exhilarating (and noisy) that I did.

Spencer is a small blond bombshell in his mid-twenties, exploding with nervous energy and constantly remembering some new point to tell me, or some new insight that I absolutely must have.

In Spencer's situation, mixed messages were the order of the day. His lover, unable to decide what he wanted, kept communicating very inconsistently with Spencer and the girl he was also having a relationship with. The result was a series of dramatic turn-abouts.

I first met Clayton in September. I didn't know it at the time, but he was then just on the point of finishing a brief, two-week relationship with someone else, a woman called Joan. What I knew was that during the autumn I would go and stay with some friends a lot, and Clayton was always there.

Just before Christmas, Kathleen, one of the friends I was staying with, said, 'Haven't you noticed that Clayton has been coming over every weekend, and never leaves? It isn't us he's coming to see, it's you, you know.'

I was astounded. I said, 'Oh, what does he want?'

She said, 'He wants to jump you.'

From then on, Kathleen orchestrated the whole situation.

The next time I was due to visit, she said Clayton might be coming round that night, so I went down there a day early. She said she had to go out to babysit, and that left the two of us together. Clayton and I talked the whole night, and then he asked me to go back to his room with him. I said, 'I thought you'd never ask.' We started living together officially on Boxing Day, when I moved in with him.

Clayton and I lived together for a year at first – I call it our 'blissfully unhappy' year.

Yet we had a good thing going. I remember lying in bed once saying, 'I'm going to love him. I'm going to love him', and I did. We were very good for each other a lot of the time. We 'built' things; he had aspirations to be a writer, I had aspirations to do art photography. Whenever we were together, there was that friendly rivalry to create something – and a lot of interesting stuff came out of it. He had a couple of things published; I sold a couple of pictures. So it was obvious it could have gone somewhere. And a lot of people then thought our relationship was something they would want to achieve, so there must have been some good there.

But in the house we lived in, there was also a woman called Joan. She was a big, domineering Irish woman, very matriarchal and yet blatantly sexual. She was married – her husband was a weed – and I didn't like her from the beginning. The first night I slept there, she came down the next morning and sat on our bed and started talking to Clayton. I thought, 'Who's she?'

Clayton told me later that he had spent two weeks with her, just before he met me. They hadn't got on all that well, and all they had had was what I'd call narcissistic sex, where he sort of lay back and let her do what she fancied. It didn't seem like sex to me.

But that two weeks seemed to have made Joan decide that Clayton was the one she wanted. She was already married, but nearly separated from her husband. She kept coming on very strong with Clayton, even when we were together. I remember we were all sitting around one night, her husband, me, Clayton, Joan and some friends, and she quite blatantly jumped on top of Clayton and started French kissing in his ear. Everyone said afterwards that they felt really sorry for Joan's husband; I kept thinking, 'What about me? I had to watch that spectacle as well!'

How did Clayton feel? He would have said that he was heterosexual with homosexual tendencies. He was coming to terms with his own sexuality when I met him. He couldn't cope with other people knowing, and he went through a stage at the beginning where he kept saying, 'I'm not gay, I'm bisexual. I'm not closing all my doors.' So in some ways having Joan after him was what he wanted.

After a year, Clayton and I moved to a house where we had separate rooms. That was all right for a while, then Clayton invited Joan to come and stay. Her marriage had broken up and she had nowhere to go, so she stayed with us.

One night, I think it was after she'd been staying with us for three or four days, she came in; I was just leaving the bedroom, and had only a towel slung round me. She was slightly tipsy and she said, 'I didn't realize – you're quite attractive.' Then she tried to jump me. I pushed her away and went out.

After that, she started to spend time with Clayton, treating him as if he were her boyfriend and not mine. She just didn't seem to get it, that I was with him. I told her we were having an affair, and she just didn't believe me.

After a while, the relationship with Clayton wasn't going too well, and I began to think that maybe I should get out for a while. Then one day I came home and she was waiting for me, looking very smug. She said, 'Spencer, Clayton and I have been talking, and we want you to know we're going to get married. So I think it's best that you leave.'

I was astounded. Him getting married? But she was so definite, and kept telling me about the plans and what they were going to do – and I wasn't getting any real answers from Clayton. In the end, I just left and went to London.

During that first three months in London on my own, I did a lot of soul-searching. I began to think more and more about him, wondering what would have happened if we'd stayed together.

I survived in London though, and then one holiday I was going back home. I got on the plane, and I'd just settled into my seat when this voice said, 'Spencer!' It was Joan. She sat there the whole way telling me how well she was and how well Clayton was and how happy they were together, then she said, 'Oh, and he's meeting me at the airport.' You can imagine how I felt.

We got off the plane and walked into the airport lounge and there he was waiting. We just walked towards him, the two of us, and he just looked from one to the other of us and back again. His face was a picture. When we met, he said, 'Hello, Spencer', and then, 'Can we give you a lift back?' So I said, 'Yes, fine.'

We drove in the car back from the airport, and I was sitting in the back seat, listening to Joan talk about their marriage plans. Now and again, I could see Clayton glancing at me through the rear-view mirror. They were going to drop me off at the pub and, as far as I was concerned, that would be it.

When we stopped, Clayton asked Joan to go to the off-licence to get something to drink. I was just getting out of the car when he grabbed me by the arm and said, 'I really need to see you before you go back. I need to talk to you.'

I told him that I was very busy, but I was willing to meet him. I told him the name of the club where I would be that

Saturday, and that I would be there all night. At first, he said he couldn't come because he would be out with Joan that evening, but I said, 'That's what you've asked me and that's where I'm going to be.'

He was there. I saw him immediately I walked into the club. He was wearing the sort of clothes we used to wear when we were together, and he was dancing with Joan. He stopped, walked up to me, brought her over by the hand, threw his arms round me, gave me the most passionate kiss he'd ever given me and said to her, 'Now do you understand? Now do you realize?'

She stormed out.

I ended up going back to his place, and we went back to London together the following Tuesday. It was one of the nicest times we'd had together, like the honeymoon we'd never had – love, not just lust. I know he used me to make a statement to her that he was not interested in any of her ideas, getting married or having children, and that was fine.

When Joan heard that he'd moved back with me again, it completely blew her brains out. The message had finally struck home. Two weeks later, he got a phone call one night from his mother. I've never seen anyone turn quite so pale. Joan had phoned his mother up and told her he was living with a drug addict, a junkie who had AIDS. I went berserk. I said, 'If that woman ever comes anywhere near this place, or phones up or tries to contact you, I'm not responsible for my actions. It's up to you to tell her to keep away.'

He managed to get it sorted out with his mother, and I don't know what he said to Joan. But one afternoon a few weeks later, we were sitting watching TV with some friends, and there was a knock at the door. I couldn't believe my eyes when I opened it. Guess who!

I said, 'You were told never to come here. Do you really think I'm going to let you over the doorstep?' I started to shake. If I'd had a knife in my hand, I would have put it straight through her. It was as simple as that. I went back inside the flat and decided that was it. It was too much to handle. It finished there.

Looking back, I think it all happened for a number of reasons. Clayton came from a very confused background. His parents used to fight a lot, and ended up divorcing, but his allegiance to his parents changed over time. One minute it was his father who was the greatest, the next it was his mother. I realized that he had created that situation again with his lovers. He found his security in the insecurity, which really is a very dangerous thing to do.

Clayton was very afraid of commitment. Even though we saw each other for almost three years, there was never any commitment longer than six months. I was asking him to choose, to make a commitment, and he was terrified of that. So he used Joan as something to protect him whenever I got possessive. Equally, if he ever felt insecure about me, he would go and seek comfort with her, though he never really told her what the true situation was.

There is a postscript. Clayton left London and moved in with a new boyfriend. I went down to see them once, and we went out for dinner. In the restaurant, his boyfriend was being really nice, going out of his way to make me feel at home, though Clayton was practically ignoring me.

Then the boyfriend said, 'What do you know about someone called Joan?' I was shattered. I told him, 'If that woman is involved anywhere at all, it's bad news.' And I turned to Clayton and said, 'How dare you do that to him, you're not going to do the same thing to him that you did to me.' But he was doing it. All over again.

From the start, this three-way dance is packed with mixed agendas and hence mixed communications. At the start, Clayton lays the foundations by being unable to communicate his attraction directly to Spencer; instead, a common friend does it for him.
    When Joan appears, Spencer takes an instant dislike to her, as

we suspect that she does to him. Their dynamic is simple — dislike finding an answering dislike, so that they move away from each other constantly. Less simple is the dynamic between Clayton and Joan, which mirrors Clayton's varying attitude to his own sexuality and at the same time stops Spencer and Joan from actually coming to blows. We can only guess what emotions are flying, what towards- and away-from dynamics make Clayton keep living with Spencer but nevertheless get emotionally drawn towards Joan.

One thing is clear. Mixed messages are the rule here, and communication is always incongruent; if something is communicated, it is never the whole story.

When Clayton and Spencer's relationship starts encountering problems, Clayton tips over towards Joan. But he is still unsure; Spencer can get no real answers from him. In the end, it is Joan who tells Spencer to leave while Clayton stands by and allows it to happen.

When Spencer meets Joan on the plane on the way back from London, we seem to hear a clear communication from her about how well the relationship is going, but from Clayton, the message is not so clear, and we sense there are problems. In a desperate attempt to break away from Joan, Clayton does to Joan through Spencer what he previously did to Spencer through Joan. He communicates what he wants to say through the other party. Joan does get the message and, at first, withdraws.

Within two weeks she is back on the attack and, shortly afterwards, Clayton has swung the other way again. Spencer is clear that it is at Clayton's request that Joan turns up at the flat the final time, and he knows what Clayton is now communicating to him.

Spencer has been through all this before. He could choose to stay in the relationship, but the communications are too intense and too incongruent. The dynamic has to flip over into a new way of working . . . he withdraws for good.

The postscript, however, shows that even without him, the spiral goes on . . .

Abigail

I rang at the door of Abigail's house and was immediately welcomed into a bustle of noise and people. We ended up in the kitchen, where one lodger was cooking curry, a teenage daughter was painting a picture for Grandpa's birthday, and a squabble was in progress about sharing out a box of chocolates. Eventually, people left, and Abigail and I set up the tape recorder on the kitchen table and started the interview, interrupted only a few times (usually at the most emotional moments) by family, friends and paying guests who tiptoed in, smiled, stepped over the microphone lead, and tiptoed out again!

A sudden and very intense emotional interaction totally changed the way Abigail's husband saw their relationship. As a result, their whole marriage began to break down. As he vacillated, trying to decide what to do, during which time he gave Abigail totally mixed messages, she eventually found a way to communicate to him both directly and effectively what she wanted.

I met my husband when I was a student nurse in London; we're distantly related and met at a family wedding. He was fun, amiable and good-natured. I was the one who did all the travelling and had all the adventures. In fact, I was about to go to Canada and had already booked my ticket when he proposed. I cancelled my flight.

We were married for a long time and a lot of it was fine, though, in hindsight, it had its cracks well before he left. He hated the fact that I worked, that I didn't really look after him properly, that I tried to be independent. He tried to 'collect' me and put me in a jam jar, criticized me constantly, reduced my self-esteem to an all-time low. For my part, I always tried to be what he wanted, but it was never enough.

Despite that, I couldn't leave. Women with children can't leave; they have nowhere to go. He didn't beat me, he gave me regular housekeeping and, in that sense, I had nothing to complain of.

It all happened in 1983. I'd been abroad on a sailing holiday. I'd had a wonderful time, full of crises and adventures and mind-blowing things. I thought that no one could have had such a holiday as I had. Albert had been on holiday as well, on a personal development course with the Open University, and I'd had a letter from him saying that he, too, had had an amazing time. He said it would take him the rest of his life to tell me about it. That was exciting, and I wondered what it was all about.

He came to collect me from the airport. He took me home and then went off to a meeting – I knew he'd be back later. Something seemed strange, so for some reason I looked through the telephone numbers of the friends he'd been on holiday with and rang up the one he'd spoken about most. She was called Rosemary. I didn't speak to her, but to her husband Tom, and we got on well, started talking deeply and carried on talking for over four hours.

What I didn't know then was that Tom knew, but did not tell me, that Albert and Rosemary had fallen in love with each other. During all that time of talking to Tom, I never guessed.

I went to bed, slept, and Albert came back from his meeting in the early hours of the morning, and came to bed. In the morning, I got up and went for my run. As I came back into the house, Albert was putting the phone down. He took me into the living room, poured me a drink and told me that it had been Rosemary on the phone. Tom had told her that he had spoken to me and that had brought everything to a head.

Then Albert told me what had happened. The holiday he'd been on had been very intense, very intoxicating. At the beginning of it, he'd told everyone what a wonderful wife and wonderful children he had. But slowly, over the two weeks, he had fallen in love with Rosemary and he now thought he wanted to be with her instead of with me.

At first I didn't believe him. I just stared, and then I shook, and then I just went to pieces. That was the beginning of three months of hell. From August to November, we lived in hell, as Albert tried to decide what he was going to do.

He would write lists of things he did and didn't like about me. He would send me flowers, and send Rosemary flowers. He would phone us both from work. He took my car keys, so I couldn't use our car; I didn't understand that, and when I asked why, he said, 'Because it's our fucking bedroom! You're always in this house, Bill's always in her house. We've got nowhere else to go.' I hadn't thought of that.

I tried very hard to keep him. I'd always tried to please him, always tried to be the person he wanted, and now I tried even harder. But in the end nothing worked; I wasn't the sort of person he wanted and he came to a point where he realized that. But then he was trying to find ways round everything, so that he could keep the house. It got to boiling point: he blamed me of course, saying that it was eighty per cent my fault, and that he had never done anything wrong.

It all ended very abruptly one evening. Albert was sitting at my desk in the living room, while I was standing nearby ironing a whole pile of shirts. He was talking in a monotone, carefully practising each word in his mind beforehand so that it wouldn't be threatening or suggestive. It was really bizarre to be talked to like that.

He was making lists, looking through our address book. I said, 'I wish you'd stop talking about it and go for good. You could afford to live in digs for a bit until you find somewhere to go. We could still stay friends.'

He said, 'No, you'll have to leave the house. I'll tell the court you've been having affairs.'

I said, 'But that's not true.' He said that whether it was or not, the court wouldn't know.

I said, 'You can't say what isn't true. You've got to leave. You've got Rosemary, you've chosen to go and I'm telling you to go.'

He went on and on about how he would tell the court that I'd had affairs, how he would stop at nothing to get me out of the house, how if he had to leave he would make sure that I left too. It was so awful, after I'd tried to be everything he'd wanted me to be.

So I hit him with the iron to stop the noise and the pain I felt.

I really would have liked him to have died there and then, though I watched in horror as the blood poured from his head. He was conscious in fact and quite calm about it: he rang for an ambulance and rang my brother to come over and get the children. The ambulance came and took him away. I just watched it all happen; I didn't feel a thing.

After he'd gone, I first scattered all the shirts I had been ironing for him round the garden. Then, I cycled over to see him there at the hospital. When I went into the ward he just screamed, 'Get her away from me! Get her away.' So I left.

I suppose Albert has the sort of person he wants now. I don't think the affair finished it; I think the marriage was over long before, but the holiday clarified things for him, disturbed him and made him realize that I wasn't the sort of person he wanted. His relationship with Rosemary is successful because it gives him everything he wants. She doesn't go out to work, so she's always there for him. She tidies herself up before he comes home, which I wouldn't have dreamed of doing. She probably gets up to give him breakfast in the morning. She's something like his mother, but good in bed.

As for my life, when Albert went I was left with an all-time low self-image. It was as if I'd become disabled by fourteen years of marriage; I was terrified of how I would cope without someone to look after me. In fact, I was perfectly able to cope. I had done lots of things, travelled extensively, brought up two children. But I had no belief in myself.

It did get better as the years went by. I read books, went to counselling, got out and met people, started to have other relationships. And I remember quite clearly the turning point.

I had caught the last train back from London and fallen asleep on the journey. I woke having passed my stop, and when I got off the train, it was one o'clock in the morning, I was freezing cold and I had no money on me. I felt very alone, but I coped. The station staff were very kind, made me coffee, rang to find out the cost of a taxi for me, and eventually stopped a train to get me back to my station! I learnt from that – that I could make my own decisions and be responsible for myself. I was OK on my own.

I just thank heaven that he left in time.

Abigail and Albert have a complementary dynamic. When Albert criticizes, Abigail gets afraid and tries harder; when she tries harder, he reacts to her fear and criticizes. It is painful for Abigail, and no doubt Albert feels that he is unhappy too – but the relationship has been stable for years. They have each responded to the other's emotions with the same emotion, time after time.

This time, something is about to change.

The flip-over occurs when Albert goes on a course. We suspect that the relationship has already reached its change-point, and this is the final push it needs to tip the balance. The introduction of a new element in the dynamic, Rosemary, is that final push.

Given the setting, a residential course with the emphasis on personal development, it is not surprising that the situation between Rosemary and Albert quickly becomes very intense. Neither of them has anything or anyone to hold them back; they are in a little world of their own, interacting, communicating, spiralling upwards.

It is fair to say that if such a communication had happened within a different context, maybe over a longer period of time, or without the emotional freedom of the course, the effect would have been different. The intensity would have been lower. Possibly, it might not have been enough to tip Albert over the edge.

Once back at home, with Abigail part of the dynamic again, Albert finds himself pulled in several directions; he is now not sure what he wants, and so he gives mixed messages all round.

Abigail tries to cope with this by doing what she has always done – trying to please him. But in the new configuration, this just won't work any more; Albert has, through his interaction with Rosemary, changed, and Abigail's previous emotion no longer raises the same emotional response in him.

More and more confused emotionally, trying not to be 'threatening or suggestive' and so succeeding only in mixing fear with his anger, Albert gives Abigail increasingly inconsistent communications. Eventually, she cannot take it any more, and like any human being faced with a series of impossibly mixed messages, she reacts in a clear and direct way. She hits him, simply to stop the pain. In fact, it is very effective because it flips the dynamic over into a new configuration, one with which Abigail can cope. Albert realizes for the first time the depth and intensity of her emotions and, having realized, has to withdraw totally, which is what Abigail wants.

Freed of the pressure of having to please all the time, Abigail now, herself, begins to change. Something catastrophic had to happen in order to stop the destructive dynamic in which she and Albert were trapped – Abigail's action was that something.

7 Intimate secrets

To tell or not to tell, that is the question. The key issue, the one which separates eternal triangles from all other kinds of intimate relationship, is this one. How much should people be told? How much do they want to know? How much do they sense anyway, even if they consciously know nothing?

This is not an issue that just affects the 'abandoned spouse'. There are things that a lover will never learn, there are things that a partner will never learn, and there are things that are hidden from both. The eternal triangle is a hot-bed of things that cannot be told, which, if revealed, will split the situation wide open.

What kind of people keep affairs secret? There is a common presupposition that only 'bastards are that deceitful'; the interviews I held showed that rather than being deliberately vicious, people who hide the truth are more commonly just afraid. If we really want to hurt someone, then we tell them openly that we have a lover when they least want to hear it; if we are afraid, we hide the truth. If you have a lover and you know your husband will disapprove, then you will keep it secret through fear of his reaction. If you still sleep with your wife, but know that your mistress would leave you if she knew that, then you will hide the fact through fear of the consequences. Whether or not we 'should be' ceasing our affairs, or 'ought to be' telling the truth, is another issue. Once we have chosen to form a triangle, then often the only way to avoid the unpleasant and frightening consequences is to keep that triangle hidden.

Often, the not-telling is justified by the not-teller in terms of what the other person 'needs' or 'wants'. 'She would object ... he would feel betrayed ... she wouldn't understand.' Certainly many of the interviewees I spoke to believed this. Particularly where a couple's agendas are in conflict, or where they have differing ideas of the symbolism of an affair, secrecy is seen as a way of resolving things.

Equally, many of the partners I spoke to seemed to have turned such a huge blind eye to what was going on that they must have chosen to ignore the facts; any other interpretation would label them stupid. What do you do if your wife comes home four hours late from work three nights a week, as Bindu did? How do you cope when your partner 'consistently misses the last train', as Robert did? You challenge or you ignore, and many choose to ignore. Some partners, aware that their spouses may take lovers, make it clear that they do not want to know, set up a self-erected block to communication that imposes secrecy on all. One woman told me, 'He doesn't mind me having affairs, but he doesn't want to know all the gory details. His view is that I can do what I like as long as I don't tell him about it.'

Many partners I spoke to claimed that it was not a question of them turning a blind eye. They never knew, never suspected a thing. Yet often, somewhere in the interview, there came a hint, a clue; yes, they had actually noticed a difference in love-making, there was a sudden change in communication. Things got suddenly worse, or suddenly better, and it did cross their mind that . . .

For even if we never allow ourselves to know in awareness, even if we never consciously spot a single clue, somewhere along the line emotions will be transmitted. It is actually impossible for there not to be any effect if a dynamic changes. As I have made clear, the feeling is always transmitted round the trio; when lover affects wife, then wife will affect husband. There will always be a knock-on effect. If we do not choose to recognize this effect while it is happening, then there will be good reasons why not – but an effect there will still be. There are subtle ways that spouses and lovers use to communicate with each other, even if they do not consciously know that the other exists; ways of using the third person as a channel of communication that is unconscious, but, nonetheless, extremely effective.

If we know what is going on, why do we not recognize it consciously? The answer lies in the same emotion that motivates 'erring' partners to hide an affair in the first place – fear. There may be fears that a challenge may tip the dynamic over too far, too fast and all may be lost. If your wife is besotted with her new lover and you discover that, she may choose him instead of you. If your lover is lying to you and you recognize this, you may have to stop seeing him. If your partner's new affair is making him easier to live with, then you may be afraid that finding that out will just recreate all the difficulties prior to the affair.

The pattern that is emerging then is certainly not a simple one. A partner who keeps an affair secret often does so because they do not want the primary partnership to end. Someone who colludes with that block to communication, consciously or unconsciously, often does so because they want to preserve their relationship intact. Should we then keep all eternal triangles secret? Is there any reason to tell the truth? It all depends on what we want to happen.

Any blocking of emotional communication has its price – because interaction will communicate real feelings anyway, and this may be far worse. If you do not tell your spouse what is happening through fear of their reaction, then the fear you feel will communicate itself anyway, and damage your marriage nevertheless. If you turn a blind eye to your spouses's indiscretions despite the fact that you are actually furious about them, then the knock-on effect of your collusion will transmit itself round the triangle, bringing anger and resentment in its wake. The harm will just get done another way.

Secrecy does not stop the emotions happening; it just drives them underground. If underground is where you want them to be, and you are happy that most of the crucial dynamic is happening on a level where you can neither see it nor control it, then choose secrecy. Keep secrets from your spouse or your lover, let your spouse or your lover keep secrets from you. Remember, though, that in so doing, you risk relationships developing and change-points occurring, without your being able to do a thing to stop them. Lovers may leave, wives may stop loving, husbands may run out of patience, and you will not be able to prevent that. If you know, you can act.

If you decide to be honest, however, and if the truth does come out, the effect will be immediate. Almost certainly emotions will rise — secrecy would not have even been an issue if there were no strong feelings to consider. People will not react calmly. Every aspect of the dynamic will speed up. Relationships will destabilize, change-points will occur, and things will alter. If you are happy with that, then tell. If not, keep the secret.

In many triangles, the truth often slips out. Lovers just 'happen' to leave tell-tale clues, husbands or wives just 'happen' to find incriminating evidence. This is almost always because the situation has already destabilized. Either things have gone too far, or someone has been pushed too far, and inevitably, change must occur. An easy way for it to change, irreversibly, is for the truth to come out. After that, nothing is ever the same.

Joanna

Joanna is an old friend. I went to see her in her country house, and sat in front of her fire talking, while her Great Dane prowled restlessly around wondering what was going on. She is tall, slim, blonde and one of those women who, no matter how dishevelled, always look sexy and attractive.

Now happily remarried, she spoke of a time when she took a lover. At first, it was ecstatic, but then the lover's wife started to confide in her — about her suspicions that her husband was having an affair. Joanna was caught in a seemingly untenable position.

I still remember it very vividly because it meant so much to me. My husband and I were mixing in a group of people of about my age — mid-thirties. I had not long ago given birth to my fourth child, so I had been entirely immersed in child-rearing and it was very nice to start talking to adults again.

I had noticed Phillip, but in a very off-hand way. For example, I noticed when we had a party for handicapped children that he was very good with them. But I really didn't take him seriously in a sexual way, just spotted him.

Then I began to realize that he was 'spotting' me, and I began to tune in to the fact that he was really rather dishy, and he clearly thought I was. He was tall and well built and that really appealed to me. That was as far as it went until one night my husband and I threw a party, to which Phillip and his wife Joan came. She collared me and started talking about how very much she wanted children and had been trying to have children for ages.

I remember not liking her particularly, but at the same time feeling sympathy for her — so I did my bit. She began to contact me a lot, and that meant that we were all thrown together. I began to feel really strong sexual vibrations for Phillip. Eventually, I felt I really had to do something about it. I couldn't think properly — I was like a teenager.

I decided I would be positive. I rang him up and said, 'I have something I must talk to you about; can you spare an hour at lunchtime?' He said he'd come the following day. I put the phone down and thought, 'Well, Joanna, now you've done it. Either you are going to have a rip-roaring affair, or he's going to slap you down. Either way something positive is going to happen.'

When he arrived, I sat him down, gave him a drink and said, 'I am fairly sure that there are vibrations in the atmosphere between us which are not good news, and I think your wife suspects. She's clearly upset about something, and I think we ought to clear the atmosphere.'

His way of clearing the atmosphere was to get up from the sofa, pick me up off the ground and cart me off to bed! That was the end of the conversation and the start of our affair.

It was all very clandestine and tremendously exciting. I couldn't have him coming to the house all the time because of the kids, and of course I couldn't go to his house. So I rang up my best friend, told her the truth and said, 'Is it possible to meet at your house sometimes?'

And she said, 'Be my guest!'

We used to meet about once or twice a fortnight, I suppose.

Physically, the whole thing was absolutely magic for both of us. I would arrive first, he would drive up in his car surreptitiously. When I answered the door to him, he would immediately seize hold of me, and we would run up the stairs to bed. It was totally engulfing, uninhibited, a current of passion that left us no time to think, no time to analyse, just do.

At time went on, though, and we got to know each other better, there began to be areas where I was aware that we weren't compatible at all. Yet I ignored this because, compared to the rest, it seemed so unimportant. I was really besotted and so was he.

I don't know exactly what the attraction was. For me, it was to do with the chemistry each time we met; the physical side of things was wonderful. I think I understand what it was for him because I have had this effect on men before. I was slightly older than he was, and I think there is an attraction in maturity and also in my image as a coper, a person who can do everything terribly well. He fell in love with the image of me really rather than me as I am.

Then, after about a month and a half, something totally devastating happened. His wife rang me up to say that finally she was pregnant. I remember saying how delighted I was, and, in many ways, I was truly pleased. But there was a cold stillness inside me. I knew that that was the end for Phillip and I – it obviously had to be.

The next time Phillip and I met, I explained that his wife had told me about the pregnancy and asked him what we were going to do about it.

He said, 'I just don't know. She's wanted this so much, but I don't care for her any more.'

We talked and talked, and in the end I said, 'I will just borrow you for a while, until the baby arrives, because I know when that happens you won't want to know me any more.'

And he said, 'What I want to do is to go through the pregnancy with her, and then I'll leave, and you and I will go away together.'

I agreed, though I didn't believe it. I don't think he realized what happens when you have a child. I've had four, so I know that when the baby is finally born, your whole attitude changes. I kept telling myself that when the child was born, he would love it and not be able to leave it – but a part of me still kept hoping.

In hindsight, I shock myself. I don't know whether I would have been capable of going away with him. I doubt it, but at the time I wasn't thinking straight. Yet I was certainly capable of deceit, of playing all sorts of roles and lying wickedly just to keep things going. I knew we only had six months left, and then it would be over.

That time in my life was very weird. Phillip's wife had a terrible pregnancy, because he was very indifferent to her. She believed it was because she was no longer beautiful, but fat and ugly; in fact, it was because he wanted to be with me and was just staying until after the pregnancy. She was so distraught, and it was me that she turned to and leant on. I spent hours reassuring her that it was all right, that men often reacted badly during pregnancy, lying through my teeth all the way. I found that I could actually change my role, and that when I was speaking to her I was no longer his lover, I was actually her confidante.

I wondered whether to tell her the truth, but then I realized that that was what I absolutely should not do, the worst thing that I could have done. I felt duty-bound to stick with it. I was never tempted to tell her, simply because of her vulnerability. I did come very close to it, but the moment just didn't arise.

I realized that what I really should be doing was finishing the whole thing there and then. But I couldn't take that decision. I was so overwhelmed with physical joy that I allowed myself to indulge in that for a while without thinking through what was happening. I think everyone's dream, if they want to be unfaithful, is that they can do it without harming anyone. And I hoped that too. And I never used anything she told me to get my own back or make life difficult for her or Phillip.

The time came for her to give birth, and my husband and I were going abroad on holiday with our children. I remember the whole time thinking about whether she had had the baby or not, and when we came back the first thing I did was to gallop to the phone to find out what was happening. She'd had the baby on the night we'd returned.

I went to see her and she was over the moon with her baby.

I also went to see Phillip, and what he said was, 'I can't leave.'

Of course, I'd known all along that that was what he would say, but, when it happened, I was absolutely devastated. Part of me had kept hoping. I did everything in my power to change his mind. I even said, 'I don't want you to leave her. That's fine. Let's just go on as before.' Yet he wouldn't. He was very unhappy because he still loved me, but he had just realized what really counted for him; he wouldn't leave his wife because she would keep the baby and he couldn't accept that.

The next year was awful. I saw nothing of him; he absolutely refused to see me. I wrote to him frequently and kept phoning him, trying to get him to contact me, but he would not.

He continued not to be able to sleep with her, to be very unpleasant to her, to drink too much. He had realized what a relationship could be like because of what we had, so he turned against her, even though he stayed with her. She was certain he was being unfaithful, and was continually threatening to leave. They were always having rows and, during one of them, he stormed out and on the way looked into the baby's cot and said, 'You'll understand one day. You'll understand one day.' There were terrible things like that going on.

She would come back to me and report all this. I let her, not only to give her support, but also because her stories helped me to feel closer to him.

It all came to a head very dramatically. She invited me out to supper one night and I went. I was really hoping I might see him when he was picking her up or something, but there was no sign of him at all.

We were sitting there in the restaurant, and all of a sudden she said to me, 'Joanna, I am absolutely certain that he is having an affair with somebody. This is just going on for so long. I know he is.'

I said, 'Have you any idea who it might be?'

And she looked straight at me, and said, 'You.'

I said, 'You've got to be kidding!' And I said it genuinely. I'd actually changed into that other role, the confidante rather than the lover.

Then she said, 'Oh, of course I am.' She knew, but she gave in. The rest of the evening was spent talking about other things.

When I left her, I really despised myself. I thought, 'You absolute pig, Joanna. How could you have been like that? There was your opportunity to speak, to be honest at last, and you didn't take it.' I think, in hindsight, though, I was right; I can't see that it would have been any use to her to know. All it would have done would have been to relieve me of a guilty secret, and I don't see that there would have been any justification in that. I've had that happen to me since. A partner told me about an affair that was over, and I wish like hell he hadn't. I'd accepted his lie and everything was all right, so I'd have been much better off if I hadn't known.

Things did change from that time on. I started back-pedalling, staying out of Joan's life and finding good reasons why I couldn't see her. Incredibly, though, she wouldn't let me go. She hung on for two years, and the only way I escaped her clutches was by moving house. She rang me the night before I was moving and asked if there was a chance of meeting up. When I explained I was moving, she asked for my address, and I said I wasn't sure of it but would write. Of course I never did. I haven't seen either of them from that day to this.

The crucial aspect of this triangle is Joanna's relationship with Phillip's wife and the secrecy they maintain between them. Already, before she is even properly aware of her attraction to Phillip, Joanna is giving Joan emotional support over her childlessness. At first, this simply allows Joanna more access to Phillip, and prompts her into realizing that she is attracted to him; then, their affair begins. It is 'clandestine' from the very start, and this itself makes it exciting. Joanna has even more tension in the situation, because Phillip's wife is also pursuing a relationship with her at the same time.

Then, Joan gets pregnant (and we may ask what the significance is of the timing, that after so many years without children, she should conceive at the very time her husband is starting an affair). Whatever the reasons, Phillip's agenda starts to change. When the child is born, he cuts himself off from Joanna completely and she is devastated. Her way out is to continue to see Joan, partly out of guilt, but also partly as a way of continuing to communicate with Phillip. But he remains in his relationship with Joan, a dynamic of pain and guilt that is nevertheless stable, as is Joanna's dynamic with Joan, fuelled equally by guilt and a longing for Phillip, and kept alive by secrecy.

Things finally come to a change-point when Joan challenges Joanna. Does she really know? Is she only bluffing? Or is the real lie the one she tells when she says that she believes Joanna is not her husband's mistress? The dynamic between the three of them is so fraught that we can see exactly how Joan has come to this point, wanting to tip things over into a new way of relating by bringing everything out into the open. Equally, when it comes to it, and Joanna's response is to deny what has happened, Joan can only meet it with an equal denial. It seems as if the dynamic has teetered back from the edge.

In fact, it has flipped over. After her inability to be honest, Joanna is unable to continue her relationship with Joan, how-

ever much she may miss the contact with Phillip. She withdraws
more and more and finally severs all links with both of them.

Why does Joanna not tell Joan what has been happening? Fear
is certainly one answer – she berates herself for her cowardice.
But she knows, too, the pain it would cause, so she is also
protecting Joan and Phillip. Phillip, having decided to stay, has
every reason to hide the truth. By her acceptance of Joanna's
answer, without query, Joan shows that she, too, is not ready for
the truth. Had they been able to talk about it, perhaps they
would have been able to develop their relationship; but, in the
event, all three of them decide to choose secrecy and this brings
the relationship to an end.

Kevin

Kevin was a voice on the phone, a Northern accent that I
enjoyed talking to for over an hour.

He was in an eternal triangle, which he kept secret for quite a
while. But then the worst possible thing happened – his two
partners met, talked and discovered the truth. When Kevin met
them, he walked straight into what he calls 'the guillotine . . .'

I was working as a switchboard operator in a hospital up
North at the time. I was about twenty-four and had a bit of a
reputation with the girls. The doctors used to say things to me
like, 'Oh, I couldn't get near you at the party last night – you
were drowning in women!' I got involved with someone who
was a nurse at the same hospital, then I got involved with
another nurse in the same group. I liked them both equally –
the problem really came when they found out about each
other!

I met Susan in the hospital canteen. We just got talking, ate
our lunch together, and I asked her out almost right away. I
was very forthcoming in those days – I worked on the motto
of 'Catch it while it's hot'! She was small and slim with long
dark hair, very quiet and shy, almost passive, and she

appealed to my protective instincts. We went out together a lot, with me taking her back home for weekends, and then going up to visit her at her home in Blackpool. It worked well.

I met Cathy at a party about three or four months later. She was very similar to Susan in looks, also small, with long hair, although it was more auburn than Susan's. She was very sure of herself, knew exactly what she wanted, and that appealed to me. I like people who know where they're going.

Cathy and I got talking when I was propping up the bar. Susan was dancing, but I'm disabled – I have infantile paralysis – so I don't dance. I certainly wasn't jealous of Susan dancing with other people; I may have been envious that she could dance and I can't, but I certainly wasn't possessive about her. People need their freedom.

Somehow, I managed to chat Cathy up and get her phone number before Susan came back to me at the end of the party. I found out that they were in two different nurses' homes, which was useful, but I was still unsure about following it all up. I hesitated, I think, not so much because I didn't want to go out with two women, but because I wanted to be honest with Susan. But in the end, about two or three weeks later, I did phone Cathy and we started going out together.

Why did I want to sleep with both of them? Well, it was a good boost to my male ego, for a start! There were other, more serious reasons, though. I'd been going out with Susan for three or four months, and we were getting very close to each other. But she had just begun to start to feel uncomfortable about getting involved. She didn't say so outright to me. I picked up that something was wrong and knew that either there was someone else or she was worried about involvement. So I challenged her and she admitted that she didn't know whether she was mature enough to cope with a relationship with someone who was disabled. She said she didn't want to finish with me, but she was feeling uncertain.

I suppose I should have just accepted what she said. I would do now, but at the time I tried to reassure her, make her feel that everything would be all right, and she saw that as pressurizing her. So I felt we were hitting barriers, and I did feel insecure.

I also think I needed to reassure myself that I could still do it, that if Susan left, I could still pull another woman. It was significant that I looked for someone who was the total opposite of Susan. I knew I could get off with someone who wasn't all that sure of themselves; I also needed to know that I could get off with someone who was outgoing and knew what they wanted. It was very important to me that I got to sleep with Cathy, not just go out with her – and I succeeded.

So, for a while, I went out with both of them. I have to be honest – it was good sleeping with two women at once. I loved it. I was never tempted to compare Susan and Cathy, in or out of bed. The only way I can compare people is when there are a lot of similarities between them, not when they are different.

Susan and Cathy were very, very different. Susan and I got on very well, and we were looking quite seriously at a future together. Although I liked Cathy, with her it was just an affair. I would never have made it with her long term. She was far too bossy, for a start! And one minute she would be loving, and the next minute you'd be scared to turn your back on her.

For a while, six months or so, everything trucked on happily. Then Cathy changed hospitals and ended up in the same nurses' home as Susan. Then, one day, I got a phone call from Susan asking me to pick her up at the nurses' home. I went round there in the car, suspecting nothing – and when I got there, Susan and Cathy were both there to meet me. I walked right into it!

Apparently what had happened was this: Susan and Cathy had got talking with a few other girls in the dining hall one afternoon, and my name had been mentioned. I had a bit of a reputation at that time, I must say! I have no idea what happened when it clicked with them that they were both going out with me, but I can imagine. Straight away, Susan rang me. The guillotine came down immediately, no delay.

I didn't really know what to do when I saw them both standing there. Susan said, 'Cathy says you've been seeing her as well as me,' and she was obviously upset. We all went and sat in my car, me in the driver's seat, Susan in the passenger seat and Cathy in the back, where I could see her through the driving mirror.

We talked and talked and got it all sorted out there and then. Cathy actually didn't seem all that upset. She found it more amusing than anything else, thought it was all a big joke – but then she was a lot less involved with me than Susan was.

Whether Susan was all that hurt, I really don't know. I suspect she was seeing someone else herself, but I have no proof of that. If anything, she seemed relieved that the pressure was off her, but I found it very difficult to communicate with her. If that had happened now, I would have been a lot more honest, but, as it was, I was unprepared and I fluffed the whole thing.

She said, 'Why didn't you tell me?' I said, 'I didn't tell you because I didn't think you'd like it – and you obviously don't!'

By the evening, we had all come to an agreement that I would carry on seeing both of them. They each knew what was happening, and I saw them both as friends and lovers. There was a definite shift in my relationships with them, though. I stayed good friends with Cathy, and after we'd stopped sleeping together, we kept in touch; she met someone else, though that didn't work out for her, either.

I carried on seeing Susan, but there was a definite change in our relationship. After she'd got over her initial anger, she was a bit relieved, I think, because she didn't know whether she wanted to commit herself to me. We drifted apart naturally; it wasn't a case of us splitting up. Eventually, she went to work at another hospital and we stopped seeing each other. I haven't seen her for many years.

Kevin begins to go out with Susan and has a good relationship with her. At first, the dynamic seems stable, a giving and receiving of trust and affection.

Slowly, however, Susan starts to draw back. She is not sure she can handle the challenges of a long-term future with Kevin, and the more he tries to convince her that things will be all right, the more she feels pressurized and the more she moves away. As a result, Kevin feels insecure, tries to make things all right, so pressurizing her even more. They enter a spiral and the change-point occurs quickly; Kevin, rather than moving towards, moves away, by taking another lover.

Cathy is a very different woman. Her outgoing nature makes Kevin feel confident, and the fact he has been able to sleep with her too helps him to feel less insecure. The dynamic between him and Susan stabilizes and for a while everyone is happy.

Things cannot stay like this, however, and one of the surprising things about this story is that the triangle is so stable for so long. Kevin has not exactly tried to choose partners with secrecy in mind. He chooses two nurses, and from the same hospital group and, when they end up in the same nurses' home, hopes that no one will notice, no one will inform either of them, and that they themselves will not realize.

The inevitable happens – Susan and Cathy meet. They act immediately, confronting Kevin and talking it through. It is interesting that although Kevin can be seen to have hurt Susan, he, in fact, reports her as being relieved – is she relieved, or is Kevin simply post-justifying what has happened? He has also chosen someone as the third point in the triangle who is clearly not really deeply involved with him, reflecting the fact that in this situation his main concern was to stabilize the relationship between Susan and himself. Had he been concerned to find an alternative long-term committed relationship, he would have acted very differently.

Should Kevin have kept the affair a secret? He says that now he would be more open. Then, he tells Susan what is obviously true, that he didn't tell her because he knew she wouldn't like it. Yet, in many ways, he allows her to know. He chooses as a second partner someone who has close contact with her and creates a situation with a very high degree of risk of discovery.

The eternal triangle has its results – Kevin gets his boost of self-confidence and is able to let go of Susan easily. Equally, the 'discovery' of the triangle gets its results – Susan is not only off the hook, but knows she is. In order for Kevin and she to feel able to end the relationship, she and Kevin and Cathy all need to have consciously faced the fact that there is a new situation. Kevin and Susan are no longer in a long-term relationship, and they begin to accept that and act on the realization.

Sasha

Sasha's story spanned three phone calls, which in this book I have shortened to one interview. In the first, she told me about her fifteen-year triangle with a man she met when she was a teenager, and her intention to finish the relationship.

In a second phone call, she told me how she did this. But the third call contains a sting in the tale . . .

It started like this. I met Alex when I was fifteen, and I thought he was wonderful, as you do when you're fifteen. For a while we were really happy together. He was good-looking, it was obvious that he was going to do well, and I thought I really loved him. I met him about two weeks after his mother died, and that is really important, though I didn't realize it until later.

After about eighteen months, he met Robyn and, although I was there first, he started going out with her. It became a real battle. I think we both thought he was ours and we wanted him and we would do anything to keep him.

Even when he was going out with Robyn, and supposed not to be going out with me, Alex would ring me and come round to see me. I'd spend time with him and I'd really try to stir things up. For example if Robyn rang up and I was out with Alex, I'd get people to say, 'Oh Alex is down the pub with Sasha.' Then she'd get really angry and they'd have rows.

Robyn tried to get her own back on me too. She went out of her way to do some very nasty things to me. I got a series of threatening phone calls and letters at home and her friends would follow me down the street and call out to me.

This went on for some time. Alex was still seeing me and still going out with Robyn. When he was twenty-one, he said to me that he thought he wanted to get married. I thought that was really stupid. What did he want to get married for? He said it was a good idea to get married, because Robyn was house-proud and a good cook. I found this an incredibly Victorian attitude, and so when he got engaged, he didn't tell me and when I asked him was he engaged, at first he said no.

When it got nearer the wedding, and even on the night before, he was saying to me, 'We've got to call it off. We must call the wedding off,' and asking me to elope with him instead. I kept saying, 'You're getting married tomorrow, Alex.'

So they did get married. On his wedding day, 2 June, he tried to ring me several times. On 4 June, forty-eight hours after the wedding, he was waiting for me to take me home from college. I opened the car door and said, 'You've only been married two days, Alex. What are you going to tell me – that your wife doesn't understand you?' He seemed very aggressive, demanding to know whether I was going to sleep with anyone else now he was married – and was very angry when I said that I probably would.

He kept saying that it was me he loved and that Robyn wasn't a good wife. So we kept on seeing each other. I'd try to hold out, but then he'd keep ringing me, or keep coming round and telling me that he loved me.

He'd lie to me. He told me once that Robyn had left him, and he wanted me to come round to his house. I believed him and I went. When I got there, we went to bed, and I left a picture of myself in the pillow case. I thought, well, if she really has left, it won't do any harm. But of course she hadn't, so the next time she did the washing, she found it and they rowed.

Alex just kept on and on trying to see me. I'd hold out, then I'd give in. Whenever he saw me he'd tell me he loved me and that they were going to split up, and I'd believe him and go with him again.

It got to a point where Alex and Robyn were going to divorce and he rang me up and took me with him to see a flat. He said that he was going to put a deposit down on the flat and he wanted me to move in with him. I said, 'Alex, that's ridiculous. I'm not going to move in with you.' He wouldn't move into the flat until I'd agreed to move in with him, and when I wouldn't, he let the flat go and got back together with Robyn.

This all went on for nine years, on and off. They would move, get a new house, and as soon as that was done, he would phone me up and we'd go back to the house and sleep together again. They moved several times.

The whole while though, I never contacted her or let Robyn know that I was around. He gave me his phone number and I think that was quite a risk – I could have phoned her up and told her everything, but I didn't. In fact, Alex kept doing things like that – giving me his phone number, taking me to his home – all of which allowed me to tell Robyn in subtle ways that we were having an affair. I remember once I scrawled some graffiti on the bed sheets – 'Cathy and Alex were here . . .' I don't know what she did when she found that.

In the end, as I got older, I thought I wouldn't put up with it any more. I moved to Israel. I told all my friends not to give Alex my address, but one of them wasn't all that smart and she did. So in the end, I got a letter from Alex saying how much he loved me, and how he wished I'd come back so we could be together. I'd then got to a point where I wished that I'd taken more from him rather than simply giving, so I wrote to him and said, 'Dear Alex, I need £150 to get back to England. Please send the money.' Within two weeks there it was, so I came back.

Then I moved, and again I didn't tell Alex my address. I told everyone who had my address that they weren't to give it to him, and that was all right for a few years. Then I got raped, and I was really upset. I didn't want to tell my Dad, I didn't know who to tell, and I thought of Alex, so I rang him. Then we were in touch with each other and it all started again.

Next came the point where I realised that I was lesbian. I really enjoyed telling Alex that, seeing the look on his face as he realized. He didn't ring me for ages, then when he did, he said, 'Oh Sasha, I've been so worried about you. I just keep lying awake at night thinking about it, and how disgusting it is.' I know he really wanted me to meet a man and get married and settle down; but I really liked shocking him by getting him to meet my gay friends. Alex often expressed concern at what he called my 'lack of shame' about being gay. In some ways, I attribute being a lesbian in part to having known Alex — it is probably the only thing I could ever thank him for.

This has been going on for fifteen years in all; for the last few years, since I've been lesbian, we haven't slept together, but the involvement has still been there. Then, about two weeks ago, my friend Bernadette said to me, 'You know, this goes on because you're dependent on Alex. What would happen if all of a sudden you weren't dependent on him, if you didn't need him any more?' Actually, things are going well for me at the moment. I'm going to buy a flat with a friend and we're going to move in together in about eight weeks. And now also, I have a man friend who wants a child; maybe we could have one together and share the costs and the childcare, fifty-fifty. So I'm beginning to realise that maybe I'm not dependent on Alex any more.

That's where we are now . . .

. . . When I first talked about this, I didn't know how it would end. But since I told my story, I decided what I should do. I rang Alex.

I told him all the good things that were happening in my life, and then simply told him that the mortgage had come through, and that I was moving. I was not giving him the address because after fifteen years I was putting an end to it all. Bernadette was right – he responded in a very distressed way when I was strong and powerful.

I said goodbye with glee in my voice and my heart felt as if the chains of fifteen years had dropped to the floor.

What were all our reasons for letting all this happen? I've thought about this a lot.

What was Alex after? As far as Robyn is concerned, he said she's house-proud and he likes that. What did he see in me? I really believe Robyn wasn't so hot in bed, not as good as I am. Also, I think that Alex and I met just after his mother died, and he confused me with his mother in some way, and then just couldn't let me go. I think that could be the real reason, that he just couldn't let me go so he kept chasing after me.

Why did Robyn do it? At the start I think she wanted what Alex could give her. Alex was really good-looking when she met him, and it was obvious he'd do very well in his job, so she went for him. After a while, Alex didn't matter; it was just that she wanted to be better than me and really beat me by marrying and keeping Alex. In many ways, she married him so that I couldn't.

Why did she put up with him having affairs? I wouldn't have put up with someone else leaving their photo in my pillow case. I think she must have very low self-esteem to put up with it. However, he'd always tell her how sorry he was, I know how he can lie and promise never to do it again; she probably believed him.

Why did I do it? It certainly wasn't to get Alex. I've always fought shy of commitment to him because I know what it would mean – cooking his dinner every Sunday as Robyn has to do. In any case, there was always a sort of emotional dance between Alex and I; if there was ever any danger of my moving away from him emotionally, he'd suggest a commitment – but if I ever showed signs of accepting that, he'd draw back.

I know that there is a big element in it all for me of winning out over Robyn. It is really a battle between me and her, and in some ways I feel my relationship with her is stronger than my relationship with Alex; it's very important to me that I affect her . . .

. . . After that phone call, Alex spent weeks pursuing me. He chased me wildly, sending me flowers, phoning me every two hours, sending me cards, asking me to go on holiday with him. He suddenly realized that I meant it – I was going to go. Yet when he had me, he took me for granted. I'm not giving in, though; I've told him I'm not giving him my new address and that this is the end of the relationship.

I wondered whether at the end of all this time I should write and let Robyn know everything. For, ultimately, I want to win.

Then I realized that though both she and he have survived a less than satisfactory relationship, they have no reason to divorce. She looks after his children; he provides for her and has affairs to fulfil his libido. They carry on.

If I were to let her know all this, and how he has behaved towards me over all these years, she might actually divorce him. Though divorce might upset her at first, she would then find as I had done that life without Alex was infinitely more wonderful and glorious than with him. After all, when I stopped sleeping with him, I discovered women, and becoming a lesbian was definitely the best decision I've ever made. Robyn would be well off after the divorce, young enough to live a good and happy life, alone or with someone else. She would have a real shot at happiness.

No, to ensure real misery, I won't write to her. Knowing them as I do, this will mean that they will carry on in their unfulfilled and unhappy existence for many more years to come. That's my ultimate revenge. I shall leave them together.

Sasha and Alex create a stable relationship, but from the start their agendas are different. So, when Alex meets Robyn, a change-point occurs, and the triangle begins.

At first, nothing is secret. It seems as if the two women are enjoying the emotional struggle, the towards- and away-from movement that they experience while fighting over Alex; if the fight were secret, there would be less enjoyment. For his part, possibly because of this, Alex is able to see both women without either of them giving up and withdrawing, for to do that would be for them to admit defeat.

When Alex chooses to marry, however, his affair with Sasha goes underground. Even though he continues to see Sasha, he must pretend he is faithful to his wife. Thus starts a secret triangle that lasts for over a decade.

Our first question must be what stabilises this relationship over such a long time? Alex obviously has his agendas met by having both a wife and a lover, and he enjoys this even after Sasha stops sleeping with him. Sasha, too, spirals upwards on the sheer pleasure of knowing that she has power over Alex, and is winning out over her rival. For her part, Robyn has Alex as a husband. They all believe they are winning.

There is always a complex interplay between secrecy and revelation. It is vital that Sasha and Alex's affair is not too open, or Robyn will destroy the dynamic totally by leaving. However, it is also important that Robyn knows that Sasha exists, otherwise the whole point of the game would be lost. So Sasha leaves her picture under Robyn's pillow, writes graffiti on her sheets, in effect dangles her affair under Robyn's nose. There are always ways for a secret affair to be communicated and still carry on!

During the fifteen years, change-points occur. The dynamic destabilizes on several occasions. Often, Alex tries to move all his commitment to Sasha, but she always moves away and he then moves back to Robyn. Occasionally, Sasha withdraws completely, but she always gets drawn back to the compelling dynamic.

Finally, during the course of the phone calls I had with her, Sasha decides to challenge Alex by standing up to him. By doing this, she changes the dynamic between them irrevocably. Instead of being passive, she tells him about all the things that are going well in her life – and, in so doing, makes it impossible for him to maintain the dynamic as it has been for so long. Though he continues to chase her, Sasha vows never to see him again.

Sasha, however, is left with the problem of Robyn. She debates whether to break the secrecy to tell Alex's wife what has been going on, knowing that to do this will probably tip their dynamic into a change-point. In fact, Sasha is wrong in her assessment. For just by withdrawing from Alex, and continuing to withdraw, she will destabilise his relationship with Robyn. Even if Robyn never finds out about Alex's affair, their partnership will never be the same, for without its third element, an element which has been with them from the beginning, it cannot function in the same way. Whether its new way of functioning will be better or worse, we will never know – and neither will Sasha.

The whole story

8 The knight in shining armour

Wendy contacted me through a listings magazine. After we talked on the phone, she asked me to go to see her, and I travelled cross-country to her terraced cottage, which has hanging baskets both outside and inside, plump sofas and acres of beige carpet.

Wendy is beautiful. She was once a beautician, and her knowledge of how to make the best of herself combines with natural beauty to make her quite stunning. Beige blonde hair, tanned skin, well-chosen clothes in shades of beige and light green set her off to best advantage.

Wendy's story is a classic eternal triangle, of the 'other woman' who starts an affair with a married man. It is full of euphoria, pain and deception – and yet in its own way it is a story of victory over impossible odds. Wendy's affair comes directly from her situation in a marriage which has slowly destroyed her self-esteem; for a while, her liaison builds up her self-love, but then as her lover recommits himself to his wife, the affair threatens to destroy Wendy anew.

Wendy

The time I'm thinking about occurred during the thirteenth year of my marriage. Things were not good between myself and my husband, Alain, who was a very moody man, uncommunicative, unco-operative, a total stick-in-the-mud. We'd totally grown apart and my girlfriend, Bridget, and I were always at the kitchen table bemoaning my life.

It was beginning to dawn on me at that time that I could

actually have an affair. Bridget had occasional ones, and so part of me daydreamed about a knight in shining armour coming to whisk me away while I was doing the washing-up. I never thought it would happen to me.

Then I joined a self-exploration course. The guy running it was called Jim. I didn't feel an immediate pull towards him, only admiration, so I was totally unprepared for what happened. One evening, near the start of the course, we had to do a game which involved pairing off with someone and simply saying 'Yes' and 'No' to each other. When Jim and I paired off, it ended up as a series of very sexual yeses and nos . . . I couldn't remember when I'd last felt that kind of wanting.

Also, it was very clear that it wasn't just a one-way thing. He felt the same. If he hadn't responded, however strongly I felt, I would never have approached him.

Then one day, my life changed. I was chatting with a neighbour across the road, and I saw a man knocking at my door. I didn't recognize him, so I popped back home to see who it was, and found it was Jim. He said he was just passing by and thought he'd drop in. He came in for a cup of tea and when we were sitting on the sofa talking he simply put his arm round me. We kissed, had a hug and a cuddle, and I said to him, 'Oh, isn't this dreadful!'

But my life changed from that moment. When he left, I felt as if something exciting had happened at last; everything, even housework, suddenly took on a different meaning. Life was uplifting and dangerous.

From that first day, I had this desperate need to hear him, to see him. We would both get into a terrible panic if we couldn't have the contact; it was incredibly addictive. It had taken me over like a drug; I needed the fix. I did consider stopping, but I didn't want to enough!

My whole life revolved round meetings with Jim. We were completely caught up with calling each other, seeing each other, or being with each other. I would tell my husband I was going to the corner shop to get some milk, and I'd run down the road, meet Jim on the corner and whizz off to the next town just to spend twenty minutes together. He would come by the shop I worked in at lunchtime, just to wave at me. He would meet me for ten minutes at night when I left work. We would snatch odd half hours before the children came back from school. Sometimes – what a luxury – he would come to my house for coffee in the morning. I stopped going out purposely so that I could stand vigil by the phone to catch his call; when it rang I would come out in a hot-and-cold sweat and grab it before anyone else got there. My whole life was spent plotting to see him for more than half-an-hour, to be with him for an evening, to spend a whole day with him.

Of course, when that happened, it was a total disaster. I had a wonderful vision of us wandering hand-in-hand, looking at each other. It wasn't like that at all. We marched round different tourist spots in London being totally miserable. When I sat in Westminster Cathedral crying, Jim asked me what the matter was, and I told him I was remembering lost loved ones. In fact, I was crying because the day had been such a disaster. I really thought he was never going to want to see me again.

Our sexual relationship began on my living room carpet. We would build up the most incredibly hot and steamy atmosphere. We longed and lusted after each other, spending hours just holding, kissing and touching. Often it wasn't necessary to have intercourse; in fact, it was two months before we actually slept together.

When we did, I took the key to a friend's flat and we stole off and used that. It was all very secret and very daring. Actually, the sex itself was no great shakes – I think we did it because it seemed like the completion, the ultimate, but, in fact, it didn't measure up to the deliciousness of the build-up. The passion was far better than the penetration! Also, Jim was riddled with guilt about his wife, and I felt it; it seemed he gave himself permission for all the bits beforehand, but not for the intercourse itself. I think he was doing it for me and not because he wanted to. In fact, our affair started well before we had intercourse, if you count the affair as consisting of the pure obsession of it.

We carried on like this for about a year. During all that time, my husband never found out. He was a very jealous and possessive person, and I would have thought he would have suspected. In fact, I didn't do a very good job of keeping it from him. I went out a lot more, suddenly had a busy social life, got very edgy about being around him. I even took phone calls from Jim at home in front of my husband. He seemed to ignore everything.

I'm sure he colluded with me. If he had admitted he knew he would have had to do something about it; there would have been arguments, there would have been a lot of pain. So he never approached me and asked what was going on, never asked. It felt as if he didn't really mind, because he was actually getting some spin-offs from it; I stopped pestering him to talk to me, stopped nagging him.

We'd had a very odd relationship, my husband Alain and I. I met him when I was living in Switzerland. I was introduced to him by some friends, and at first we didn't really get on – he didn't speak English, only a little German. We went out one evening and I wasn't all that struck, but he pursued me.

One day he asked me what I was going to do that night. When I said I was meeting a guy at the disco, he immediately slapped me round the face. I thought, 'God, he must really care about me' – and I fell for him from that moment on. In the background I'd come from, you see, being hit meant being loved. He was very strong, very manipulative, ten years older than me and something of a father figure. He simply took me over.

By the time I met Jim, things were different. I was aware that although sex with Alain was brilliant, something big was missing from my marriage – emotion and softness. I used to get very depressed. I remember one Remembrance Sunday I couldn't stop crying, and Bridget was ever so supportive, while my husband just went out and cleaned the windows. He had no idea how to handle emotions.

Just before I started the affair, there had been a change in my relationship with my husband. He had always been a father figure to me, very protective, but also very strict, going into violent fits if things weren't clean or the house wasn't spotless. Recently, I'd realize that however much I did around the house, I couldn't make ours a happy family, so I thought, 'Sod it, why should I bother,' and I began to back off and let him take over. He'd suddenly taken all the housework off me completely, just leaving me to look after the kids. That led to my spending more time with Bridget, my friend, and conversations with her led to my realizing just how shitty my life was.

Then I started my self-exploration course. That opened up a lot for me, made me realize that I wanted to be close and safe and intimate with someone. When I met Jim, I saw him as the missing bit of the jigsaw that I needed: the emotion, the loving. There was, I'm sure, an interplay between my finding my own independence and my taking a lover.

Jim's situation was very different. He was happily married – and hadn't had any affairs before he met me. In fact, he said at the beginning that he loved his wife, but was merely fond of me. He really laid down the ground rules about our relationship, which made me feel very rejected. He said, 'I'm going to be very honest with you; I don't want you sitting on my doorstep.' That really hit me; I said, 'How dare you even think that! I wouldn't dream of sitting on your doorstep.' I have to be truthful – I was infatuated, but, at bottom, I felt I didn't want it to go anywhere either. I was married, and though I had a difficult relationship with my husband, I had never positively thought of getting out of it.

Why did Jim have an affair? Some friends reckoned, knowing

his wife Christine, that it was because I was much more bouncy and buoyant than she is; she's a very lovely lady, but unexciting. I seemed more fun, more exciting, more spontaneous, more overtly sexual.

Jim did agonize over having an affair. He suffered guilt over sleeping with me – and I was so obliging to him. I saw him when he had the time, I moved only when he said so. I'd say, 'Oh, it doesn't matter. If you can't see me, it's OK.' I was so shit-scared that he would call it off, that I used to say, 'No, no, I'm fine! I'll just take these ten minutes here. It's all right if you want to spend the rest of the day with your wife.' I managed his feelings in a way, kept them safe.

Also, with monotonous regularity, he would say, 'I don't think this will work.' When things got really difficult for him, when he had had enough of being at home with her and wanting to be with me, then he would say to me, 'I just can't cope with this. I'm too in love with you.' I would think that was stupid and would make all kinds of excuses why he should just see me when he could. I would say, 'We're not doing anything wrong. We hardly ever make love, just enjoy each other's company. What's wrong with that?' I'd talk him out of leaving, time and time again.

Then, Christine found out. Jim left some romantic writing lying about one night as he went to bed, and she found it there when he got up early the next morning. She confronted him, he phoned me and said, 'We've got to talk.' It was all very sudden; he came and picked me up in the car and we talked it through desperately.

At first, things seemed optimistic. He would discuss things with Christine and come back to me saying, 'I think it's all right. She says it's all right for me to be friends with you.' I'd think, 'This is marvellous – what a lovely wife.' Then, after a while, when they'd talked a bit more, he'd say, 'No, it isn't all right. She doesn't like it.' She used to think about it and get worried. Then they would talk again and she would be reassured. That was the cycle, the ritual, on and off. She even came round to see me at one point, and asked me to leave him alone.

Eventually, Jim said we must finish it. I begged him not to cut me off altogether, but he said he had to, because, 'When I see you, I want to see you more.' So we arranged to spend a morning saying goodbye. We went to my friend Bridget's house and got into her bed and made love and then said goodbye. It was awful, gut-wrenching. When he left he was crying, and I was howling my eyes out.

I went back home and totally cracked up. Bridget took me away for a weekend in Bournemouth and I even wrote Jim's name in the sand. For two months, I didn't see him, just exchanged music. He would send me tapes of beautiful, slow, piquant music we'd heard in the group together, and I would spend hours lovingly recording music for him. My blood and guts went into those tapes. They were the only contact I had.

One day, about two months later, though, I was at the swimming pool with my children. I looked up and there were Jim and his wife. She came over and gave me a big hug. Then she said, 'I'm getting out of the water now, Jim. Are you coming?' He said, 'No, I'll just stay in the pool for a minute.' So he stood in the pool and we held hands while bobbing around. He said really beautiful things to me, but then she was there making faces, so he got out.

I got out too and went to lie by the kids' pool. She came over and said to me, 'I was prepared to let you and Jim see each other again as friends. After seeing you together in the pool today, I know you're still in love. It shows a mile off. So I'm sorry, but no way.'

I was desolate again. My mother, who was in on the whole thing, took me to America. Jim wrote every day, and I wrote to him. I was still absolutely obsessed.

It all started again the minute I got back. Jim phoned up and told me he was now ready to see me as a friend. Of course that wasn't true; the minute we saw each other we knew it would start again. We went on exactly as before, except I think it was even more profound. This time, it lasted for a year. Christine knew we were meeting, but she never knew how often, or how intense it all was.

I did feel guilty, all through that year. I felt guilty about my husband, and about his wife. I felt particularly bad about my children and the way it affected them. My son didn't find out what was happening until the very end, when we were divorcing, but my daughter came home one day and found Jim and me on the living room floor together. She went upstairs, and I followed her up and tried to explain that nothing was going on. She said, 'Rubbish! The whole street knows you're having an affair!' I tried to deny it, but of course she didn't believe me. It must have been a bad time for her, a surprise to find out that Mum wasn't the person she thought. She went through a horrendous adolescence, totally rebellious, and I think my affair did affect our relationship in some way.

In the end, after a year or so, Christine put her foot down again. She issued an ultimatum that if our friendship didn't stop, she was leaving. Jim didn't want that. They'd been together a long time.

So one day, he came to see me in the morning before I went to work. He said, 'Look, Wendy, it's got to finish. Christine can't take it. I can't take it. I don't think you can take it any more. It has to end.'

I went to work feeling so angry with him, both for finishing it at that point and for finishing it anyway. We'd been through all that hell before, and now he was finishing it. I couldn't wait for the day to be over so that I could march round to his house and talk to him. I was full of energy, though I didn't know what I would do when I got there. I can still remember the total energy which got me round there, the energy fuelled by an anger I'd never experienced before.

I knocked on the door and he opened it. I said, 'You can't just come up to me and say it's over. You can't do that to me.' We walked over to the field at the back of his house, hand in hand, and talked about it. I really got angry. Then, all of a sudden, his wife came out, and said to him, 'Your dinner's ready. If you're not there in five minutes, I'm throwing it at the wall.' Then she turned to me and said, quite kindly, 'You look really ill, Wendy.'

I said, 'Sit down with us.'

'I won't sit down. And I won't be part of this triangle. Your dinner's ready, Jim. Either come home and eat it, or . . .'

That was the finish. Something happened to me, I had crossed over some sort of threshold, felt different from that day on and I didn't want it this way any more. Three weeks later, I petitioned for divorce from my husband. That was painful and took a while, but it was for the best. The children in particular blossomed after it – and so did I.

Jim and Christine are still together; they have a commitment for life. They know each other so well; they've come through so many difficulties together. They have an arrangement that he can still see other women if he wants to, as long as he doesn't have a sexual relationship with them. My opinion is that he misses not having an affair, misses the feeling and the intimacy. I think he also liked being fought over, having two women who both wanted him. I think, too, that he's very wary of affairs; his compromise now is to try to connect in close relationships that are non-sexual.

Christine hated our affair so much because she was upset that she didn't get what she wanted from him. That is always where complications arose. If he spent time with me, he used up all his energy and his closeness and went back feeling low. She felt I had all his intimacy, the intimacy she wanted.

I don't feel angry towards Christine now; I never did. At the time, I never really wanted him to leave her, never really wanted him for myself – otherwise I would have fought for him. I was always pleased that he had Christine at home to look after him.

It was right that I petitioned for divorce when I finished with Jim. I was heartbroken, but I felt so angry and hurt that he'd finished it that it gave me courage, fuelled me to get out. I realised that I couldn't keep on in my marriage, live without being in love; it just wasn't enough. I wanted more, I wanted intimacy, I wanted love.

Jim and I have worked very hard over the past years to turn our sexual relationship into a good friendship – it was hard, but we did it and I'm proud of that. Now we see each other regularly and spend good times together. I never wanted to end up with Jim, though I would never have been happy with him. He was more of a bridge to what I really wanted.

Trapped in a relationship originally based on her idea that love must show itself in violence in order to be real, Wendy begins to change enough to want to break free. Her agendas in choosing Alain as a husband have now become eroded; the dynamic between them, at first positive, has become one of mutual disillusionment.

When the story begins, things have already begun to destabilize. When Alain berates Wendy for not looking after the house properly, Wendy's response is to become even less efficient. As she becomes less efficient, he berates her more. When Alain takes from her the responsibilities she has, Wendy's response is to feel even more invalidated and even less responsible. The spiral moves onwards; Wendy is pushed out of her own home almost entirely, and begins to have the time and the energy to look elsewhere.

Her agendas in doing so are not entirely unconscious. She knows she wants gentleness and warmth, she knows she might even want an affair. When her self-development course gives her back just a little of her lost self-esteem, she becomes able to go for what she wants.

Meanwhile, Jim is in a worthwhile, but slightly dull, marriage. We will never know the precise dynamic, the exact relationship with Christine that allows him to want an affair. We will never know just what his agendas are, although we can guess. Whatever his precise situation, when he meets Wendy, he feels able to act, and she responds.

What follows is a classic loop of mutual attraction. Wendy quite rightly says that it is Jim's attitude that leads her on, just as it is her willingness that creates his attitude. The 'yes' and 'no' game is only the beginning. Very quickly, the emotions intensify.

What stops them spiralling continuously upwards? What prevents them rushing off into the sunset together? Almost certainly, Jim's relationship with Christine stabilizes what is happening. For as he gets more involved with Wendy, as she moves forward and makes more demands, so his emotions for Christine draw him back. In response to this, for fear of losing him, Wendy draws back, allows him to keep it all safe; Wendy is quite right when she says that she 'managed' his feelings.

Equally, the situation between Wendy and her husband does not erupt. As Wendy admits, despite her passion, she has no agenda about a committed relationship with Jim, nor does she want to hasten the spiral so that they can be together. Also, despite the evidence, Alain does not challenge Wendy about Jim. The change in their dynamic is pleasant enough for him to want to keep things stable; and his fear of the alternative is sufficient for him to pull back from a direct challenge. Whether or not he consciously knows what is going on, we never find out.

Things remain stable for about a year. Then, the inevitable movement they have set up in their dynamic tips them over. Jim is being pulled more and more towards Wendy, yet he knows he wants to stay with Christine. His communication to both of them is confused and incongruent – the result is inevitably distress. Christine must, by this time, have noticed the change in him. He 'inadvertently' leaves some writing lying about, which Christine finds. With this revelation, things can only change.

A new dynamic begins. At first, it is unstable, tilting this way and that as Christine at first feels threatened and then reassured. Interestingly, for her, as for both Jim and Wendy, it is an interplay between the symbolism of the affair and the reality of it that is both distressing and positive. All of them see it at some point as having positive aspects; but, in the end, the reality of Wendy's 'having all the intimacy' means that Christine feels disturbed. Faced with the evidence of their emotional attraction during the meeting at the baths, Christine moves firmly into feeling threatened, and Jim moves with her into breaking up his relationship with Wendy.

Given space and time away from her, however, he (and Christine) feel less upset. When Wendy returns from America, the whole thing begins again and repeats itself for another year. Again, neither Jim nor Wendy leaves their partner, again they keep a spiral of attraction going in a controlled fashion, moving towards each other and away in a dance which never quite resolves itself.

It does evolve, however, and once more Christine's emotions go over a threshold. Jim again pulls away from Wendy and we will never know if he seriously intended to go through with the proposed break-up. This time, however, both Christine and Wendy are at a change-point. Christine is threatening to leave, Jim is backing off, frightened, and Wendy, flipped into real anger for the first time, takes charge and ends the relationship.

Her resolution and her renewed self-esteem also allow her to resolve her marriage. Once this is done, she is such a different person that she can not re-enter the affair. More than that, she does not need to, for her unconscious agenda of ending her marriage has been fulfilled.

Wendy speaks of the affair fondly. Its reality was vibrant and exciting, its symbolism lay in her being carried off by a shining white knight. But once she has made the emotional move away from Jim, her agendas change and the affair has to die away, even if only slowly. Now, she finds it all 'a bit tedious' and recognises Jim's place in her life as being over. She has moved on from her old situation, and she no longer needs her stepping stone.

9 She would rather not know

Catherine is an athletic, blonde and irrepressible lady. She is divorced, and lives with her daughters in a wonderfully haphazard house in a garden city in the south of England. When I visited her, she showed me a black and white photograph of Carl, a handsome, gaunt man staring straight into a camera. Catherine herself asked Carl whether he would talk to me, and I interviewed him by phone a few days later. A few weeks after the interview, I got a chatty note from Catherine, and enclosed in it was a copy of the original advert that created this particular triangle.

Carl and Catherine
Carl

I am a research chemist and happily married. My wife Ann and I have always been very clear that we are committed to having full-time careers. We both work in specialized areas, which makes it quite difficult to get two jobs in the same place, so we've ended up with her in Bristol and me having a job in London.

What I did was to get lodgings just around the corner from the office and stay there a couple of nights a week. It's actually very convenient, but on the whole very lonely. I have always had a more active interest in relationships with members of the opposite sex than Ann has – so I advertised. I explained the situation: that I was happily married, that I was looking for a companion, but a lover as well. I was quite clear in my own mind that I was looking for a lover.

Ann doesn't know at all; I haven't discussed it with her at any time. I know she would be offended and hurt if she found out, because I have had previous affairs and, when she got to know about one of them, she was offended.

I put my advert in. I got one reply – Catherine. I regard this as first time lucky! Her response to me arrived on the morning that I was due to fly to Japan on business, so I took her letter with me and scribbled a reply to her at the airport, as I was getting on the plane. Then I got in touch again when I returned a fortnight later. We phoned, we spoke, and she invited me up to her house to go to the theatre with her.

I have very clear memories of first meeting her. I travelled up after work and arrived in the early evening. I remember so well the warm welcome, the bustle, the daughters running about. When it came to going to the theatre, Catherine had double-booked her evening. She didn't fuss, simply handed me the tickets and said, 'You go off and watch the first play and I'll join you when I can!' That was wonderful; I was immediately attracted by her easy spontaneity.

I was sure I wanted to sleep with her that first night. We didn't in fact sleep together then; both of us decided that on principle. Somehow, though, I knew that we would make love. Somehow I knew that Catherine was the sort of person who would enjoy sex and be happy to do it. I think we slept together on the second night we met, though we didn't spend the night together because she didn't want her daughters to know. Since then, we've never looked back; that was about a year ago.

We see each other once a week, occasionally twice. The real joys of the relationship are many: the excitement, the adventure, the exploration. I enjoy being in her house, helping her; sometimes I take my tool box round and do jobs for her. Sometimes I help the girls with their homework. This is enormously rewarding for me.

Also, the sex is very good. Catherine takes enormous joy in

sexuality, loves to give and receive pleasure, and that gives me pleasure. At the grand old age of fifty-one, for example, I have just discovered that I can still have genuinely new sexual experiences. When we are making love, Catherine enjoys being on top because she can control what we are doing so as to give her the most amount of pleasure. My role is more passive, and I was absolutely delighted to discover recently that when we are in that position and Catherine has an orgasm, I can actually feel her contractions. That told me the pleasure she was experiencing, and so I experienced it too. It was a revelation to me that many people throughout their lives never experience, and to me it is a genuinely loving experience.

In return, I feel that I have given Catherine enjoyable experiences for the first time. I believe I've let her be herself, to ask for what she wants. We really do communicate about sex; we talk about it a great deal.

I don't feel tempted to compare Ann and Catherine as regards sex, but it is sometimes inevitable. I have a wonderful relationship with my wife, but sex isn't the main component of it. Our sex life together started well, and was very active when we first married – though even then I always used to take the initiative. She never used to suggest we make love, never used to give any overt signals for initiating sex; I think she just never developed any opening gambits. Also, we don't talk about sex. When I try to start talking, she changes the subject, not maliciously, but simply because she isn't interested. It is just as if we were talking about golf, which she isn't interested in either.

I sometimes think about Ann and whether she knows about my affair. I'm certain she suspects, but I'm sure she would simply rather not know. If she knew, she would have to challenge it and stop it. If she doesn't know, she doesn't have to do that. In fact, she benefits a lot from my having a mistress; Catherine keeps me generally young and on my toes! It's more than that, though; as I said, Ann and I have agreed to have separate jobs and so, to some extent, separate lives. We've talked about it a great deal, and we're happy with this, but it means that we live a very hectic existence and Ann simply can't make time for the kind of relaxation I get with Catherine. Equally, if I wasn't getting a regular sex life with Catherine, I wouldn't be able to give Ann the kind of non-sexual cuddles that she really values. She enjoys being very close, and we put our arms round each other every night when we go to sleep. I'm sure this would not be possible if I wasn't enjoying a regular sex life.

Ann and Catherine have met. I really wanted Catherine to know about my family and my life, so on one occasion I asked if she would like to meet Ann. We went to a naturist club that I'm a member of; once a month or so we all meet at a local sports centre and play different sports, go roller skating and it is generally a very sociable event. So I suggested to Catherine that if she really wanted to meet Ann, she come along one month.

Along came Catherine, and purely by chance ended up in the queue next to Ann. They actually played badminton together, in the nude! I watched the two of them and could hardly keep a straight face. Afterwards I said to Catherine, 'How on earth did you manage that?' It's just like her; she has a terrific sense of fun. Ann didn't say a thing afterwards, except that the woman she'd played badminton with was very good, but that she couldn't actually remember her name.

The only thing that does concern me about any of it is the furtiveness; I would love Catherine to know my family and all about my life. I know beyond any doubt, though, that my relationship with Catherine is no threat to my relationship with Ann whatsoever.

In the future, of course, things will change. They have to. Catherine is getting older, her daughters are growing up. She may well want to remarry and, if she did, I would wish her all the joy in the world; the companionship of the married state is wonderful and I myself could never do without it.

The only reason I would bring the relationship with Catherine to an end is nothing to do with Catherine herself, but to do with geography. Catherine doesn't live near my work, even though that was one of my original criteria in placing the advertisement. It gets very awkward and tiring sometimes running a triangular existence and how Ann accepts that I spend one night a week away from my lodgings every week, I don't know.

I hope Ann never finds out. I wouldn't tell her about Catherine spontaneously, but if she wanted to know, in a spirit of genuine friendship and concern, I would find it hard to deny it.

My relationship with Catherine is immensely rewarding, but I wouldn't want to swap her for Ann. And Catherine knows that.

Catherine

I met Carl through an advertisement which said, 'Happily married man in London on business two days a week needs congenial company to enjoy time with.' At the time, he thought he just needed a friend and I was looking for friendship, too, since my husband and I were divorced. It appealed to me.

I replied, but Carl was just flying off to Japan. He wrote me a scrappy note saying, 'Just off to Japan. Let's meet when I come back.'

It was Drama Festival Week in town here, so I asked him to come to dinner and an evening of three one-act plays. By the time he came to dinner, though, my daughter had told me she had a college event on and needed a lift to get there and for me to be with her. So when I opened the door to Carl and saw him standing on the doorstep, I said, 'The good news is: dinner's ready. The bad news is: I can't come to the play.'

We had dinner. My daughter and I whizzed off, and in fact I got back in time for the last of the three plays. Then we came back home and talked and talked. He seemed amiable and is tall and thin; I was absolutely charmed by him. When it came to the end of the evening, I said he had better go home, and he said, 'I told my landlady I wouldn't come back; it's too late now.' So I made up a bed for him in the living room.

After that, I rang him up again and asked him to another play. He began to come every week, and he has done ever since.

He's immensely kind. He takes me shopping, mends things around the house, loves making things work. Early in our relationship, he helped one child with some electrical problem, took the other one for a driving lesson, floated Lanterns for World Peace with me on the City Lake, and took me out to dinner. And that was all in one night after work.

We see each other here mostly, but occasionally I risk it and go up to his house, when his wife is away. Also, he goes up every six weeks to see his mother who is chronically ill in hospital; I meet him and go too. She doesn't know who he is, so she doesn't know who I am either. It can be a really grim day for him, but it's better if I'm there. We stayed overnight once in his mother's house, in an unaired bed in freezing weather. It was uncomfortable – but the sex was great!

The sex is always great. Technically, Carl is the most satisfying lover I've ever had, and that means he finds me very good in bed, because he takes such good care of my needs. We do have an amazing sex life; at the moment, for example, he's been very ill and, last week, he was worse than ever. I went to visit him at his home – a big risk – and the au pair answered the door. So I pretended I was the district nurse. She said that Carl was asleep, and so I said, 'Could you make sure he's asleep, please, as I have to write it in my report!' She went up to see him, and he was awake and asked her to bring me up to his room. She went out and I stayed; even though he was so ill, we made love twice!

I knew he was married from the start; his wife knows he stays here and has even rung here for him on one occasion. To her, I'm just his landlady one night a week. She's a workaholic and very successful in her career; they had their children late, so she's in her forties with two young children, and a job! Carl's very happy with his family, and his wife. The only thing is, she hasn't got time to play, while he works hard but likes to play too.

I've met Ann. I've even played badminton with her. I enjoyed myself so much at that evening! I was as high as a kite, roller skating naked! As I was getting my ticket at the door I got talking to a chap called Richard, who introduced me to some women and we made up a four for badminton. While we were playing, Carl watched, and I only found out later that he did that because one of the women I was playing with was his wife and he was curious about who Richard could be.

After the badminton, I remember that I went to have a jacuzzi and because I was with Richard, Carl was able to come and talk to me. He couldn't resist talking to me which was nice, and when I left the club I found a note on my windscreen from him saying, 'I love you, Catherine.'

I have no desire at all for Carl to leave his wife. I wouldn't want to spend seven days a week with him, though it's so great when he is here. My biggest priority at present is my daughters, helping them grow into mature adults, so any man taking up a large space in my life would have to be accepted by my daughters too.

My relationship with Carl meets all my requirements, and is great fun, very close, caring and sharing. It's the ideal situation.

Carl and his wife have an established relationship. Their agendas in life are similar, they prefer the same day-to-day life. They both work to the full at jobs they enjoy, sharing family life, having a warm and deep friendship.

When it comes to sexuality, however, they differ. From a positive spiral of mutual arousal at the start of their marriage, they have somehow moved into a pattern of less sex and less excitement. When it comes to the symbolism of taking lovers, they differ totally in their views. For Carl it is a light thing, a way of expanding his life and his experiences. It is not a way of finding someone else; he is very clear about that. He is happy with what he has, but he wants more.

Ann sees things very differently. She finds the symbolism of affairs a threat, an offence to the marriage – and previous experience has shown Carl that if she knows he is having an affair, she will object.

To fulfil both his and Ann's agendas, Carl therefore chooses as a lover someone who does not want to get involved with him, and whom he can keep secret. To Carl, this secrecy is fairly acceptable; he would prefer openness, but, with his conflicting agendas, settles for secrecy and a lover rather than openness and monogamy. Certainly his wife, even when faced with Catherine in the same room as her husband, does not seem to notice what is happening. Carl himself believes that Ann does know on some level, but consciously prefers to ignore the truth.

Catherine is the ideal lover for Carl. She enjoys Carl's company and his love-making sufficiently to want a stable relationship with him. Neither the symbolism nor the reality of the relationship is a problem to her; she joins in the secrecy of the affair with an excitement that spurs Carl on.

Catherine is safe. She has agendas of her own about not getting involved, about prolonging the enjoyment as long as possible without tipping it over into emotional intensity. She has no problems about Carl's being married, and is never tempted to pull him away from his wife.

It is this particular dynamic which keeps them all stable. Carl keeps his marriage as his primary relationship, and it seems from what he says that he would never give up Ann for Catherine. Equally, Catherine has no agendas constructed around having him as a full-time partner. Both are happy with this arrangement. Perhaps the only thing that could threaten their contented dynamic would be Catherine finding someone – or, of course, Ann finding out.

10 Leaning
on the lever

At first glance, this seems a straightforward story. Jane and Stanley were married for many years; it was a stable relationship and, as they approached retirement, they were looking forward to their final years together. Their huge house in London would be the backcloth for a comfortable old age surrounded by children, grandchildren and assorted animals.

Then Jane had an affair. It began as a light, easy fling, and ended when she got involved, Stanley got very hurt, and her lover's wife issued an ultimatum. Stanley and Jane's relationship slowly broke down, and now they are separated, living in the same house but on different floors. Stanley lives alone, Jane has a new, younger lover.

Is it all Jane's 'fault'? She gambled her marriage, just as it neared its fulfilment, by a pleasure-motivated fling ... and she lost the gamble. But I discovered that the story is not quite as simple as that.

When I visited them, I talked to Jane first, climbing flights of stairs to her light, bright top-floor flat which she shares with a lodger. Jane is in her mid-fifties, a fine-boned, tanned woman with fair, greying hair, wearing soft, loose clothes in bright colours. She stopped working a few years ago, and now travels a good deal in America and Europe, staying with friends and 'working her passage', as she puts it, by counselling and teaching. Her room is piled with striped mattresses, books, posters, cards and beautiful mementoes of her travels.

Jane and Stanley
Jane

I met Stanley about twenty-five years ago. I was living alone at
the time, with my baby daughter Linsey. Life was tough and
the place we were living was bad, very damp. One of my
friends said, 'I'll get you Stanley's number; he'll do the
decorating for you.' I think she also thought he might take me
to the pictures!

When he first came round, and I opened the door, I practically
fell over; he was so gorgeous. He gave me flashes of so many
people who had been important in my life – previous
boyfriends, my Dad . . . I didn't think in terms of going to bed
with him at all, though; I was thinking in terms of the
decorating first and foremost! In the end, we did sleep
together, though it took a while.

It worked very well. He was separated from his wife and
missed his little girl dreadfully; I had Linsey, he used to
babysit for me, and that brought us together. I had a child and
he had a child, and that was the basis of the relationship; in a
way, it was not about him and me at all.

When it came to relationships with other people, Stanley was
clear right from the start that the only thing that would allow
him to be totally monogamous would be a piece of paper and
a formal marriage contract. I respected that. I knew he had a
fairly casual relationship with a woman named Joan – a
once-a-week thing. She was a career-orientated sort of person
and didn't want a long-term relationship at the time, so it
worked quite well for her. We both knew about each other
and at first it didn't bother me in the least. For myself, I was
monogamous; before I could really be happy about sleeping
with Stanley, I'd gone up to Nottingham, and cleared a lot of
things with the man who was Linsey's Dad, to make sure it
was all really finished.

Then Stanley and I decided we wanted to have a child. We

tried, and almost immediately I miscarried. At the time, Stanley was working for Joan and was staying there for several weekends. I'd started having the miscarriage before he left to go to Joan's that day, and then I carried on and had the miscarriage, and it was twins.

I was totally alone and desperately upset and really needed him to be there, so I rang him at Joan's house. I said to him, 'I've had the miscarriage and it's twins.' I suppose I gave him the facts and he responded in kind – but I wanted him to drop what he was doing and come round straight away, which of course he didn't. He didn't seem to be very interested; I felt that I'd done the wrong thing in ringing him. If I'd been clear and asked for support, maybe I would have got it. But I believe – or I certainly did then – that if I'm in trouble, then I'm on my own. I don't get help.

I got pregnant again, and we had our first child together, with Stanley still seeing Joan. Very soon after, I became pregnant again, and this time I got even more distressed about him not being there a lot of the time, so I gave him an ultimatum: 'If you want to fuck around, then fuck around. If you want to be in a relationship, then I'm here.'

He left me.

It was winter time, and our baby was due to be born at the end of July, so he was gone for most of that pregnancy and I was desolate. I wrote to tell him that if he wanted to come back, it would have to be before the baby was born, because if he left it until afterwards, that was it. I wouldn't want to know and he needn't bother coming back.

He left it until the very last moment. He came back the very day the baby was due. I clearly remember him sitting there, on the edge of the sink, saying, 'You're not such a rotten old cow after all. Perhaps we ought to get married.'

In fact, I wasn't all that interested in getting married. I was delighted to see him back again, but I couldn't see the point of marriage for the sake of it – for me, marriage was because you wanted to be married to a particular person. Stanley's angle was that he wouldn't enter a committed monogamous relationship without it. I took a few weeks to decide, not because I didn't want him – I wouldn't have had children with him if I hadn't been sure – but because I wasn't clear about his reasons. Eventually, I said yes.

We went into the marriage knowing that it wouldn't be all sweetness and light. We did work at it. We were both very committed to the children and to our family life. We did an enormous amount of work on this house; we had the roof off, fixed the plumbing, completely redid it. We had a good sex life too – I was always very happy to make love, even if I was half asleep in the middle of the night! And I certainly was in the relationship for ever and ever, until death do us part, and we were both completely monogamous while we were married. It was a good partnership.

After twenty-two years, Stanley was ready to retire. Our youngest child had left home and we were planning our life together. He was going to take over the housework for a while, until I retired, and then we were going to go travelling and do our own projects, individually and together, perhaps even live apart for a while. We planned to spend the last few years together, with the children gone and more money for doing whatever we wanted.

For quite a long time, Stanley had been saying he would quite like it if I could have sexual relationships outside our marriage. At the time, I thought what he was really saying was that he wanted to have other sexual relationships and that quite frightened me. Now I think he wanted to be a voyeur; I guess he was turned on by my being attractive to someone else.

There was someone from work who was sexually interested in me. That's unusual for me. All the time I was married, I had virtually worn a label saying 'unavailable'; even when we had a very attractive young man lodging in the house for a while, I saw him only as a son. But my 'unavailability' didn't stop

Gene making advances to me – and it didn't stop me being turned on, even though I didn't actually like it. One day, I gave him a lift home and he started kissing me and touching me. I was furious, but, at the same time, really aroused. I came back into the house and set upon Stanley, who thought it was the best thing that had happened to him in a long time!

I checked out again with Stanley whether he did want me to have sex with other people and he did. So I rang Gene to say, 'I'd like to have a relationship with you,' and he was delighted at being propositioned like that. We met several times in the park during the lunch hour to discuss and negotiate what we wanted; something very separate from our family relationships but that was also beneficial for those relationships.

At the beginning, Stanley was really thrilled by what was happening. He used to cook us candle-lit dinners, serve them and go away to leave us alone. He would make us a lovely little nest of a bed to sleep in. It felt weird, but it was nice and I enjoyed it. And it didn't seem to threaten my relationship with Stanley at all. The sexual relationship between us continued and was good – if anything, it got better than before. He used to leave me little notes on my car when I was at work. In fact, for the first time, Stanley fell in love with me when I started an affair. He had never told me before that he loved me.

Then, something happened. Gene wanted to go to an art exhibition with me. I thought I would check with Stanley first, and he said jokingly, 'Well, I don't know about that. It's one thing to sleep with someone else, but to go to an exhibition with them is something totally different.' In fact it was – because that's where we really started to relate to each other. The relationship developed into something very different from what I'd ever had with Stanley. I'd skive off work to meet Gene, we'd write to each other a lot, go away for weekends. The sex became very good, the only time in my life when I've consistently come just with straightforward fucking.

I couldn't communicate to Stanley what was happening. Gene and I started to exclude him, and that wasn't what he wanted and not what he'd bargained for. At the time, I didn't think there was any problem. I really believed that the relationship with Stanley was so good that it seemed to me to be absolutely rock solid. There was literally no point where I thought or felt that if I carried on with the relationship with Gene, my relationship with Stanley would go downhill.

What actually happened was that Stanley got very angry. Once, when we went to the cinema, he hadn't enjoyed the film, and when we came out and I got in the car to drive, he said he would walk all the way back alone. When he came in he went completely berserk. He poured a can of paint over me, over the floor, over the books, everything. He smashed a huge mirror. I remember saying to him, 'What are you destroying?', and I remember that, at the end, both of us cried.

I simply hadn't understood what was happening, which was that he felt distressed that I was having a relationship with someone else. I'd blocked it out because I was having a good time. By that time, though, it had all got too serious; I had got too involved and changed my loyalty. I had a relationship with Gene that was much deeper than that with Stanley, and it just made the whole thing too intense, too unbalanced.

Then, just after Christmas, everything came to a head. Gene had never been really clear with his wife what was happening. He had insinuated it, but she didn't really want to hear what was going on. However, in the end, she did know and she didn't like it. Gene and I went on holiday together, and when we got back, he got an ultimatum from his wife telling him either to stop seeing me or to move out.

I didn't jump at the chance of our being together. I knew that Stanley and I had for a long time been thinking of living separately, or doing things apart. But I always saw myself as ultimately staying with Stanley, even though in many ways my commitment was no longer to him. Equally, I knew Gene was very dependent. I didn't want him dependent on me; so I told him that if he did want to live with me, we should at least live separately for a while.

In the end, he had no intention of leaving his wife; in hindsight, that was obvious from the beginning. He made no moves to leave, right up to her deadline. Instead, we had a series of long conversations, spread over the course of a week – they all fade into each other now – and, at the end, he said that he was going back to her, but that we could carry on seeing each other, although we had to be 'more discreet'. That really didn't work for me. I couldn't have a relationship based on deception.

So Gene left for good. I was deeply in shock. I cried a lot, I was miserable all the time. Stanley was quite supportive, but he actually wanted me to cheer up and get on with things rather than work through what was happening. The other thing that was difficult for him was that I didn't want to sleep with him any more. I couldn't, I was mourning.

I still tried to establish with Stanley what we could do to redevelop our relationship, and we went to marriage guidance. What I didn't fully realize was that he really wanted us to split up; I was trying to work at reconstructing the partnership we had.

Stanley and I grew more and more apart after that time. In the end, he gave me a written ultimatum. About four months after I had finished with Gene, and just before a weekend when I was taking an important exam, he left me a note saying he wanted to separate. After that, things were really over.

I began to travel and we had the house altered so that we could each have separate living space, and that is the way it is now.

I am sure that what broke us up was that I was no longer committed to Stanley, no longer loyal to him. Had it been otherwise, I would have been able to work through everything, and it would have been all right. But for me the commitment just wasn't there, and that was what broke us up.

Stanley

On a lower floor of the same house lives Stanley. The impression here is of a house divided, the rooms partitioned, the furniture left over from the original family home. Stanley himself is a tall, slim erect man in his sixties, with a tanned, florid face and white hair. He made me tea and offered fruit to eat, then sat in his high-backed armchair to talk. The pace of the conversation was slow, steady, and thoughtful. The conclusion was absolutely not what I expected to hear.

To understand this, you have to understand that I have always grown up with altruistic concepts. My most powerful emotions are duty and loyalty, and I have been formed by those. I don't fight people for things. I don't like to hurt people; I want all about me to grow, develop and be free.

I still remember Jane's voice, phoning me from a call box when we very first spoke to each other. Voices affect me strongly and Jane's didn't please me, so at first I thought, 'She's not for me'. My first marriage had broken up and I was doing odd-jobs to supplement my income, which had been reduced through maintenance payments – and to have some company.

A friend had put Jane in touch with me; she had just moved into a room in Archway with her child, and it needed a lot of work doing on it. When I saw the place I thought, 'Jesus, this is a disgusting, stinking slum.' There was no hot water, cold water was another floor away, it stank and the glass was falling out of the worn-out windows. I so admired Jane's courage and independence in living there.

I was also glad of a bit of companionship and the odd meal. I was young, especially for my age (as I am now), and though I was sexual, I didn't really know how to approach females; I didn't want to hurt anyone. So when we came together sexually, it was through Jane. I sleep badly, and I would wake and, by agreement, phone her to talk; she was one of those people who understood me. One night we were talking and she said, 'Come round here.' I thought, this is too good to miss. So I went round, and got in bed with her – of course. That was the beginning.

I had another relationship at the time and I was open about it with Jane, but it was artificial and peremptory, not at all satisfying. It was a long-standing relationship, but it was purely sexual. I knew that the relationship with Jane was the best of the lot; it gave me more than sex, it gave me companionship.

Then the children came along. I thought it was very strange that a woman would sleep with you and have children with you and not ask for any commitment in return, but I went along with it. She never asked me for any commitment that I remember.

Left to myself, I thought that I might just have wandered off and drifted around. I didn't want to let the side down, though; I stick to people through loyalty and duty. So, at one point, I went to see Jane. I have a very clear memory of sitting on a deep, wide sink she had in her room. I said something to the effect of, 'If you like, we'll get married. But let's put it on an honest basis.' As I spoke, I sat back and the sink was wet and cold. I remember that vividly.

I was working on my wedding day. I suddenly said to the chap I was training, 'Would you be my best man? I'm getting married today.' He thought I was joking, but I wasn't. We went back and changed, my mother-in-law got some carnations and a ring and we got married. Afterwards, I got in the car and went straight down to Heathrow airport to pick up Jane's friend's son, and a few days later I went on a previously arranged holiday alone to Spain for two weeks, as a stand-in driver. The marriage was a straightforward business contract to make sure I stuck to my obligations.

Looking back, I think Jane would have liked something different, a nice wedding, a honeymoon, some affection. She put up with it because she loved me. She doesn't show her feelings much, but she said she loved me. In any case, if she had shown her feelings, I would have run away, because I'm frightened of feelings; I feel imprisoned, possessed, afraid, and yet I need people.

The marriage worked well and I believe Jane got a great deal out of it too. I don't believe in love, but it was a very good marriage and I was one hundred per cent faithful to Jane. We had some tremendously happy times. It was held together by the family and the house, by loyalty and duty, and I have no complaints. When I look back, I feel tremendous satisfaction and gratitude – but sorrow when I failed.

I have to say that when it came to a one-to-one relationship, by the end there was nothing there. It was a soft prison, that's all, and I stayed in it because of my loyalty; it was natural for me and not a conscious thing.

Then Jane's affair started. I still remember the occasion. In the background somewhere there was someone trying to persuade her to go to bed with him. I imagined that it was some young man who was sexually attracted to her, and that she was flattered.

There had been a time, a few years previously, when we had had a young man staying with us, and we had had a passing conversation about how he needed a good sexual relationship with a woman; he reminded me of myself at his age, so lost and alone, wanting female company but not knowing how to break the ice. I wouldn't have minded her sleeping with him, but Jane hadn't wanted that. It left me aware that I genuinely did not mind. I don't own anybody. Jane gets a tremendous amount of pleasure from sex and I actually like the thought of sharing something good.

So when one day in bed many years later Jane mentioned this

person Gene, I said, 'Well, it's up to you whether to go ahead.' I remember writing in my diary that day, 'Could this be the beginning of the end?' At the back of my mind was the thought, 'If so, so be it. I'll be losing something, but so be it.'

Jane started seeing Gene. I was very good to them. They had their own room here and I made them quite comfortable. I condoned and supported the affair. I wanted her to be happy.

Or rather, I wanted her to be happy and then come back to me. When on occasions she failed to come back on time, then the pain began, terrible pain. I remember one occasion when Jane had gone somewhere with Gene, I decided to fit some car radio speakers in her car. It was a horrible job, tedious and laborious, and I got very irritated. It was well over the time when Jane was due back that she phoned to say they were going somewhere else and would be even later. I exploded. I was so angry. She did come back eventually, and then I felt guilty that I had spoiled her pleasure. It was a total paradox.

Another time we went to the pictures. I wasn't sure whether she really wanted to go or not. The idea of going was to get us to communicate again, but it was a total waste of time; we just couldn't talk. We came out of the cinema and I got furious. I walked away from her in anger; I wanted to reach her, get through to her somehow. When we got home, I was seething; I did an awful lot of damage to the furniture and shouted and raved and stormed. It was the first time I'd behaved anything like this. Jane just curled up like a frightened child.

Also, I thought Gene was worthless, a sexual adventurer. The first time I saw him, I was amazed. I'd had this notion of a youth; I was flattered to think he was attracted to Jane. Then I realized that he was an older man, and that was a shock. I began to think of him as attacking our marriage, that Jane had not stepped out of her marriage, that he had stepped into it, and that to me added to his worthlessness. To me, a marriage is sacrosanct.

As I saw them falling in love, I felt very sad. I saw Jane was in love with Gene, but at the same time she would leave me notes saying, 'You have my real love'. I didn't want to rob her of what she was enjoying, but I have very very few friends, so Jane was the only real friend I had. When she was missing, there was no one at all.

During our marriage guidance sessions, Jane said that they would have run away together, but I had been so upset that she couldn't do it. If I'd have known, and if I had had a friend to support me, I would have let her go. I feel sad now in case she has missed out on a worthwhile relationship.

I never told Jane that I wanted her to stop seeing Gene. I wanted her to be happy, though I knew at the time that that was a sign that I didn't really care. I felt as if I had lent someone a book from my bedside and they had really appreciated it, far more than I did, and then kept it. I was unable to appreciate Jane's love, but the fact that Gene did and was keeping her hurt me.

Then the whole thing with Gene started coming to an end. Jane said she'd stopped seeing him, then he rang once or twice. I have no idea who finished it, only that it was over. I know Jane suffered incredibly and I did my best to help.

At the same time, our relationship was dying slowly. There had never been a strong life there; I didn't want to be there, and my heart wasn't in it, but it was as if I was travelling to a far country. I was crying because I was leaving my home, although I knew I would be less unhappy or even happier when I reached the other side of the world.

We went through two years of marriage guidance and that helped tremendously. It put the brakes on the splitting up. If you go down a slope too fast, you burn yourself and you land with a bump at the bottom. Marriage guidance helped us through that; I found it terribly upsetting, but very helpful. There was no way it could help the relationship survive. Jane was really turning over the garden to get it to flower again.

What she didn't know was that there were no seeds there.

Now we are separated and living separately. I am retired and I feel I have been spared an awful future that I see some men trapped in – a future of washing pots and going to the shops on Saturday. Instead, I have started sailing, skiing, going away. I have tried parachute jumping. It is late in my life, but I feel better late than not at all.

I've become more selfish recently; I try to get things for myself. I've dropped my notions of loyalty and duty. I have changed. I now don't try to please others; I am prepared to exchange assets to get happiness.

I'm glad it's over. It could have been quite a destructive break and I don't think it has been. It couldn't have happened any other way, I don't think. I couldn't have had an affair, because I couldn't bear to be at fault. It would have seemed shabby to have a relationship outside marriage. I never like to hurt anybody and it would pain me to be disloyal. I have to be as straight as possible.

If Jane hadn't had her affair, eventually I would have exploded. I would have become a morose, crabby individual because I would have been living a false life. So it let me out. Now, as she goes all around the world, enjoying her freedom, I feel envious of her many connections. If I had been able to listen to Jane, the re-arrangement of our relationship would have been much better; her outlook seems more mature and wider than my own.

The affair was a lever. All I did was lean on it.

The emotional shock that this story gives is centred around the different viewpoints that both Jane and Stanley offer on what happened. Jane claims that her lack of commitment broke up the partnership; Stanley claims that he unwittingly used the affair to get what he wanted, an escape from his 'soft prison'. Of course both of them are right.

The relationship is founded originally on a number of

dynamics. Jane and Stanley's agendas are very compatible; both want stability, both want children; they enjoy sex with each other and work to build a life together.

When it comes to marriage, things are different. The symbolism of marriage for Stanley is that it means he now owes loyalty and duty; affairs are his freedom, but if he is expected to be monogamous, then the only way he will agree to that is if he makes a formal contract.

For Jane, it is important that the reality of life with Stanley is stable and that he doesn't 'fuck around'. Her experience of his relationship with Joan is negative; he is not there at the times she really needs him, and she does not want a relationship if that is the way it will be.

Up to the time of Jane's ultimatum, Stanley and she have a stable relationship, but his affair with Joan makes it a not totally satisfying one. There is no secrecy, but there is unclear communication, and eventually Jane has to cut through everything and present him with a choice.

This alters the dynamic, but it does not do so until the very last day of the deadline. At first, Stanley seems to move away from Jane, but then as the time of the birth of his child nears, his emotions change and he returns. When he does, it is to offer her a choice: they can marry and have a monogamous partnership, or not marry and he will keep his freedom.

Jane takes her time to think, but decides to enter the contract. It is a business-like arrangement which takes account of Stanley's agendas and Jane's. The reality of the relationship is at times tough, but the symbolism of their contract keeps them together and working at bringing up a family.

Time passes. It is significant that just as the last of their children leaves – and the possibility of their agendas changing arises – the real instability starts to creep into their relationship. Previously, Jane had not seemed available to other men; previously, no one had approached her. So, although it seems as if Stanley is the driving force for her to have an affair, it is a result of their dynamic just as much as their original marriage was.

Jane begins to have an affair with Gene. What is his agenda? It seems to be to form a relationship, and have the excitement, sexual contact and affection of an affair; but we must ask whether he ever really considers leaving his wife. Equally, when Jane and he first come together, we know she has no thought of leaving Stanley.

Stanley's agendas are still forming. Both had agreed to spend time separately, but as the affair takes hold, and Stanley becomes more separated from Jane, his desire for her first increases and then, when he starts to feel he is no longer the centre of her world, he withdraws from the relationship.

The affair continues. At first all is stable. Jane is able to enter the relationship because of Stanley's approval. He is buoyed up by the fact that he is 'sharing something good'. But as Jane gets closer to Gene, their dynamic becomes more intense and more influential and they develop a mutual attraction that soon becomes far more vital and important to Jane than her low-key, life-long commitment to Stanley.

Stanley senses this. He cannot cope with it, and gives off inconsistent emotions ranging from support to rage. Jane is driven away, and finds even more positivity with Gene.

Why does Jane never end her affair? Because she never believes her relationship with Stanley is in danger. Why does Stanley never ask her to stop? Because he has a mixed agenda in wanting the affair to sever the emotional connection, and also in genuinely wanting her to be happy.

Stanley has almost no other way acceptable to him to end the marriage. He says himself that he could not hurt anyone; simply walking out or having an affair are alien to his nature. He therefore has to choose this convoluted way of easing himself out of a situation that now has no value. He switches his commitment from one hundred per cent partnership to no commitment at all.

Had Gene been prepared to leave his wife, perhaps Jane would have begun to spend more and more time with him, though we know that because of his dependency, she does not want to live with him yet. But when the relationship between Jane and Stanley starts to break down, and the situation begins to be different, Gene retreats to the safety of his marriage and Jane is left to pick up the pieces of her own. She says that she never saw herself as splitting up from Stanley, but after such an intensely emotional relationship with Gene it is difficult for her to return to a humdrum relationship with Stanley.

For his part, Stanley is now glad to push for a separation, which he does. In his own mind, he is now justified in ending the marriage and spending the last years of his life in the way he wants to. He returns to his earlier desire not to be married, the independence of twenty-three years ago.

The relationship ends sadly. For both there is still a great deal of unhappiness, and certainly no hope of a reconciliation. Yet in their own way, both Jane and Stanley have gained a new life.

11 Only we can split us up

Kate is in her early forties, and a professional business woman. Her partner, David, is a freelance artist, and they have lived together for several years. During a summer activity holiday in the Caribbean a year ago, Kate met Julian, who is twenty-eight. They slept together, with David's full knowledge and approval.

What are we seeing here – the end of a long-term relationship or the beginning of a *ménage à trois*?

Kate, Julian and David

Kate

I had absolutely no intention of having an affair when I went on holiday.

I'd decided to go because I felt that I was getting too dependent on my partner, David. We're very close, and sometimes I can't bear to be away from him. Even when I booked the holiday I found myself trying to cancel it, and when I got to the airport, we sat in the departures lounge for about an hour while I cried and cried waiting for the plane.

We did talk about what would happen if I wanted to sleep with someone on holiday. We've always, from the beginning, said that we didn't demand monogamy from each other, but, personally, I've not been attracted to anyone since we met, so it hasn't been an issue. David did have an affair a year or two ago, and although I got quite insecure about that, we were both very clear that our relationship was in no danger.

I found it quite difficult being on holiday. The setting was idyllic, a beach in a hot climate, blue sea and golden sand, good food and wine, and lots to do all the time; there were about seventy of us, a fairly cohesive group all doing various 'alternative' activities like yoga and drama. I did miss David, but I could handle that. The real problem was that there were very few other people on the holiday who I really got on with. One or two of the men there seemed to be attracted to me, and in fact I was uneasy about that; I was friendly to them, but very much kept them at arm's length. I spent a lot of my time on my own.

The first week I was very attracted to a French guy there. One evening, a group of us ended up singing and playing the guitar, and when in the end I got up and went out on the patio, he followed me. We went for a long walk on the beach for about two hours and talked and talked. It was then that I started to realize that I wouldn't actually mind having a cuddle. I was very clear that I didn't want to make love with him, but a cuddle would have been nice.

Then something happened that really shocked me. This guy asked me how old I was, and when I told him, and we worked out that I was several years older than he was, that was it – no more rapport, no more nice conversations. I was very angry about that. He had been attracted to me, the me he saw and spoke to, but once he found out the age difference, he felt threatened.

One night after dinner, I was sitting on the balcony watching the dancing, quite happy, but still very aware that there was really no one to talk to. I remember saying to myself, 'Before tomorrow I'm going to find someone who really understands what I'm talking about.'

Julian was sitting beside me. I have to be honest; I hadn't noticed him until a few days before when we'd done some drama work and he'd acted the role of a very powerful character. Suddenly he'd taken on a whole new dimension and I remember being quite intrigued. Afterwards I'd forgotten him.

He turned to me and said, 'Do you find you have much in common with anyone else here?' and it was as if he was reading my mind. Looking back, I think I never would have had an affair with him if he had not said that.

Two days after that, I was sitting on a rock looking at the sunset, and Julian came up and sat beside me and we started talking again. All of a sudden, it was really nice to be wanted and to want someone. I did give him very clear signals that I wanted to move the relationship on to a sexual level, because, I think, I knew a relationship with him would be no threat to my relationship with David. I had had a glass of rum, but I certainly wasn't drunk. I knew exactly what I was doing.

I remember very clearly checking out mentally whether David would mind. He had said that what was important to him was whether any such affair was what I wanted, and not dangerous to us. I knew that being physical with Julian was what I wanted, and I was also clear that there was no danger. I wasn't aware of choosing him deliberately to prove I could attract a man even younger than the French guy, but I can see that might be true.

We went down to the beach that night, talked, kissed and cuddled. It was very magical, dark and soft and warm in the sand, with stars overhead and the sea at our feet. We didn't make love, or anything near it, though we ended up naked; in the morning, I felt totally exhausted, but more alive than I'd felt throughout the holiday. We spent the next two nights together on the beach, exploring some safe things, but we still didn't make love.

Then we went back to England. I know we could have stopped it there, and I also know that I had made up my mind not to sleep with Julian until I'd checked it out with David. When I told him, he seemed quite happy with what had happened. So then I had to make the decision myself whether or not to go ahead.

In the end, it wasn't just to do with sex; I felt, and feel, very fond of Julian as a friend, too. Also, I know that had David not been supportive, I could never have done it; it wasn't that I just went ahead regardless. I'm not aware of there being anything missing in my relationship with David, let alone looking for that with Julian; but my affair did change my long-term relationship, because I think I got more secure within myself and that changed things.

I started actually sleeping with Julian about a week after we came back from holiday, each time going back to his flat and spending most of the night making love. He was very into 'a different thing every night', which was a bit of a culture shock after so many years of making love with just David. Each time we met Julian had dreamed up a new variation, and seemed taken aback that I enjoyed everything.

At the start of our affair, the sheer difference of being physical with him was enough to turn me on. I remember feeling very different about my body after our first night on the beach, far more beautiful than I had for ages. After we came back to England, and started making love properly, things changed. I began to feel I had to try to get turned on, in order to please him, and I also got deskilled. With David, I am actually quite passive in bed and he is quite dominant, and that is something that suits us both, whereas with Julian I felt he expected me to be very active, and sometimes I actually didn't know what to do. I'd lie there stroking or sucking or whatever, thinking, 'What on earth do I do now . . .'

The other thing – and I feel I'm being unfair by saying this – is that David and I know each other very well and I always know I'll come, one way or the other, even if I have to bring myself off. Whereas I did get quite frustrated because Julian didn't know the things David did, and because I didn't myself feel that I could ask for what I wanted. I remember him saying to me that he got irritated by my 'trying to come', to which my reply was, 'Look, it took me five years of "trying" to be sure of my orgasm, and many women don't ever have one.' I do feel that he was lucky with his former partner; they were both virgins, young and in love, which means they probably just jumped in and enjoyed it from the beginning.

I was not, and am not, aware of my affair having anything but a good effect on my life with David. We would make love happily and with no difficulty when I returned from seeing Julian, and we would talk things through on the occasions when I had had a disagreement or row with Julian. At first, I didn't really trust that David would remain happy with what was going on, and kept checking out with him. I remember him being angry once, but that was when I came back quite upset because Julian and I had rowed, and I think David felt powerless to comfort me, and so got angry.

In the end, it all stopped after Julian, David and I all went to a party together. I suggested it, but, in fact, I found that when faced with the two of them, my first loyalty and attraction was to David; I kept turning to him and wanting to be with him. It wasn't that I didn't like Julian, but all of a sudden the sexual energy was gone. I think it might have lasted a bit longer if the two of them had really got on with each other, and I could have fed the affection I felt for Julian with the knowledge that David liked him. But as it was, although there was no obvious bad feeling, they just didn't gel.

In hindsight, I doubt if things could have lasted much longer anyway. Or rather, I think that we'd all got what we needed.

I know that Julian could have gone on sleeping with me for a while longer, so there was still a sexual need within him. But I think our continuing friendship has met a lot of the need – certainly it wasn't all about sex, for either of us, and a lot of it for him was, I think, first about having his self-esteem boosted and secondly about having a woman friend he could confide in and trust. I think, in the beginning, when I was looking for someone I could be close to, so was he.

I think what I got from it was the change in me. I've certainly been a lot less dependent since, and a lot more sure of myself. I got the cuddles, plus I got the ego boost and the company.

And I'm sure that my having the affair helped me to understand David's having an affair.

He has always been the one to hold out for the ideal of an open relationship, and I know he saw what I did as giving him permission to have an affair if he wanted, though he hasn't had one since. I think what he got from it was seeing himself as someone who could stick by what he believed – which is that we can enjoy ourselves with other people and still love each other.

I have to say I think it might have been different if I'd have really fallen in love. But I wasn't after that; if I had been asked to choose I would unhesitatingly have chosen David. But I think I unconsciously set it up so I never had to choose, to have all the various benefits of an affair without any of the problems.

Julian

I met Kate just over a year ago on an activity holiday in the Caribbean. The holiday was advertised as 'holistic', providing activities promoting physical health and self-expression, and I went on it both to unwind and to meet like-minded people. The ads indicated the place was popular with singles and I went with the explicit hope of having an affair.

I'm generally quite shy, so I was hoping that the atmosphere of the place would lower my inhibitions and that the activities would provide a structured way of getting to know people. In a drama group I was cast in the lead role in a romantic scene and I picked the woman there that I fancied most to partner me. Our friendship began there.

I can't remember what attracted me to Kate originally – probably her child-like enthusiasm. She was obviously intelligent and full of common sense. I remember being impressed that she was proud of being more intellectual than her contemporaries, that she was experienced at counselling, and that she had her own business which employed other people. She was also fourteen years older than I am and living with another man back in England.

The friendship became an affair a few days later. We'd been watching a beautiful sunset and getting drunk on rum when the conversation turned to free love. She asked, 'What are people who advocate free love like as lovers?'

'I can only speak from my own experience,' I replied.

'And what are you like?'

'Let's go down to the beach and I'll show you.'

If she hadn't made it that easy it might never have happened.

She'd made it clear that she was in an open relationship and that she'd come to the Caribbean on her own. In the circumstances, I was willing to try my luck (she even assured me that David, her boyfriend, was smaller than I am and not into martial arts!). I think I was desperate to re-establish proof of my manhood. In a way, the age difference and her other commitment were an advantage, otherwise I might have felt that there was more at stake and would have felt far more threatened.

For the rest of the holiday we continued to take part in the activities with others, keeping a low profile on the affair during the day, and sneaking off to the beach at night. The physical side of the relationship went very smoothly; Kate was willing to say how far she wanted to go and I was happy not to push too much further.

My attention was obviously having the desired effect. 'My body wants you,' she said, on the morning of the second day, and 'I consider myself a good lover, but with you I feel like an amateur.' Such power was a big part of the turn-on for me. The affair was only the second I'd had, coming three years after a break-up with someone I'd lived with for a couple of years before that.

By the end of the holiday it was obvious that we wanted to continue seeing each other back in England. Kate said that the most important part of the relationship to her was the good sex, and I agreed with that. David provided a lot of emotional support and physical closeness, but seemed to be more familiar than exciting.

Kate made it clear that she would tell David about the affair as soon as we got back home, and that his approval was necessary to anything that happened after that. It was also clear that her first loyalty was to him, the longer established and stable relationship.

Back in England, we met and slept together eight times over the following three months. Each occasion followed roughly the same pattern; we'd meet on a Friday or Saturday evening and go for a meal and perhaps to a film before returning to my flat for the night. On the one hand, I hankered after a regular love life, but on the other hand, this relationship was more about exploring sex.

The first night we were together, I had to persuade her to stay over. The return to England had made things look less certain, away from the 'magic' of the Caribbean. We had penetrative sex for the first time and celebrated with champagne. She had powerful orgasms – loud enough to make sure that the girl next door, whom I fancied, knew about it as well.

The second time we didn't bother to go out. We went straight to bed and talked and fucked all night. She told me frankly what she liked – a slow, irregular rhythm – and in return fellated me in full view of a mirror.

On the third night, we were fucking on a table, urging each other on. She was coming down on me like never before, and unashamedly masturbating. By this stage the sex was so powerful that we had lost our sophisticated veneer, to the extent of saying, 'I love you' – it was the only worthy thing to say.

The fourth time, the strains of working life were more

noticeable; she had backache. Eventually passion returned and I tongued her to climax. She came down hard on me then, her breasts dripping with sweat.

The fifth time I provided a pornographic video, but in fact the relationship had moved on to a new level. We had agreed it was safe to stop using condoms and for the first time I felt we were really 'making love'.

The sixth time, her back was still troubling her. She wanted space to be more moody; we admitted our dissatisfactions with the affair so far. It was a first minor crisis, but, when reconciled, we reached near-simultaneous orgasm, and her strongest climax yet.

The seventh time we tried a different approach: slow, meditative music and an ultra-relaxed fuck.

The eighth time I bought her a waist chain . . . and accepted her invitation to come to a party and meet David.

I hardly spoke to him, but seeing us together freaked Kate out. The next time we met, she said she no longer wanted to sleep with me. She'd somehow compartmentalized the two relationships, but seeing us together had changed her perception of the situation. Her mind was made up; there was little I could do but accept gracefully that the affair was over.

Having said that, it had never been clear where or how far our relationship was going. How long did we expect it to last? Both Kate and I were becoming more concerned about being able to stay good friends in the longer term, and I consoled myself that it was as good a time to stop as any.

What was good about it? Her frankness and her easy-going manner are wonderful, close to an ideal I didn't expect to find. I also find her easy to trust. She seems to know her limitations, and she's dedicated to making her relationships fulfilling.

The downside of the affair came from the stresses of life, worrying about work or not being well. I refused to see her when I had a cold, which she almost took as a rejection.

Wanting her attention when she was suffering from back pain was a frustrating experience for me.

We have remained good friends since then, though we meet less often as she has moved. She says she has lost interest in having affairs with men other than David; if she did sleep with anyone again, it would just as likely be me.

I don't know what effect I had on their relationship. For me the affair was . . . an oasis of physical intimacy, a reminder of my previous affair, a confirmation of how I'd changed since then, an indication of what is possible, a boost to my confidence and the start of what I hope will be a long-term friendship.

A final point; my previous relationship split up with bad feeling as my lover rebounded with a mutual friend. This new affair was a chance for me to prove to myself that three individuals could handle powerful feelings coming up for each of them. I'm not sure whether we succeeded or whether we wisely called quits before anyone got hurt.

David

I need to set all this in a framework. We've always aimed for an open relationship. In theory, I have always felt that I had no objection to Kate's having an affair, and would always defend her right to. In practice, I have a notion of a 'worthy lover' for her. If I imagine her making love with another guy who's bright and good-looking, then that is a really good image. I'd hate her to have an affair with a big fat slob, a man with a beer gut. But I don't have any revulsion about the thought of her having a lover *per se*.

I don't think I get jealous. For me, the issue is about feeling in control of the situation. If I've given permission to Kate to have an affair, then I'm in control, whereas if she made eyes at a man in a restaurant, the fear is that he would come over and chat her up and she would leave with him and then I would be humiliated.

I'm more scared of humiliation than of losing her, because I don't think I would lose her to another man. I don't directly have experiences of losing things to other people; I have experiences of losing things in and of themselves. In my childhood, my experiences aren't of people coming up and taking my penknife, but of my coming home and finding I'd lost it. So I think that if Kate went off with someone else, it would only be possible if our relationship was weak to start with – and it isn't.

When Kate went away on a summer holiday without me, I didn't really think about her having an affair. My clearest memory is of her really wanting to talk about what would happen if she did, and my getting irritated, a really strong 'so what?' feeling. At that stage it was all so hypothetical, and I really felt I wanted to defend her right to have an affair if she wanted to.

When she came back I was really pleased to see her. I met her at the airport, very early in the morning, and then we took the car over to Greenwich and parked and ate early morning croissants and drank orange juice. I said to her, 'I presume you didn't get off with anyone then?' and she said, 'Well, yes, actually I did.'

I was surprised. Thinking about it, I was surprised partly because I hadn't picked up any tension from her when we met, and partly because before leaving she'd been so wary of having an affair. I might have given her permission to have an affair, but she hadn't given herself permission. What I'd forgotten was that when you're on holiday everything is very different, and you can make a lot of changes.

My other reactions were surprise, intrigue, some sexual arousal. It sounded as if she'd had a really good time. I thought: this is a sexual woman I'm with. That was a strange thought, because I knew she was sexual; I'd been sleeping with her for years, but it was as if sleeping with me didn't make her a sexual woman, but sleeping with someone else did.

I did feel a bit threatened. I can't bring to mind what the specific fear was; I think it was the thought of her going off and seeing Julian one day this week, then two days the next week, three days the next week, and then not bothering to come home. If that had happened, I don't know what I would have done. She did give me reassurances, but of course neither of us really knew what would happen. The only thing that could reassure me ultimately was for it to be all right in the end.

The weekend after Kate came back from holiday, she saw Julian again. That weekend was important for her because she had penetration that time, but, in fact, she's always laid far more store by penetration than I have. If she was going to have sexual contact with him, then it didn't actually make a lot of difference to me whether she had penetration or not.

Then, for about three and a half months, she kept going to see him every second weekend or so. My main memory is that over that time both our relationship and our sex life got better. As soon as I saw that the affair had stabilised and that it wasn't a threat to our relationship, then it was fine. It wasn't something that I was massively emotional about either way, but it was fine. I didn't think, in theory, that I would want to fuck her right after she'd been with another man, but I did. Sometimes, when she came back from being with Julian, I would be in bed, usually quite turned on, and we'd make love.

Sometimes she'd come home upset about him, and I was able to give her a lot of support. I think she felt she couldn't talk about him to me because he was her lover, and ultimately she expected me not to be able to handle it. In fact, there was only one time I flipped over into anger and that was only because I felt helpless to help her; I'd tried everything and she was still upset. When she said, 'I don't need to be cheered up, I just need to be allowed to cry,' then it was fine and I was able to cuddle her again.

In November, we all found ourselves at the same party and

that was a bit weird and a bit strained. I didn't have any way to get talking to Julian. I suppose I could have gone and actually made contact with him, but I didn't, so I must have been distressed about it.

When, after that, Kate said that she wasn't going to sleep with Julian again, I just waited to see. Kate is very black and white in her thinking, she doesn't say 'perhaps' or 'maybe', she always says 'will'. If I'd been in her shoes when she decided not to sleep with him, I'd have said, 'Well, I'm not so sure – things are shifting'. She said, 'Well, that's it'. But she could equally well have come back after seeing him next time and said, 'Well, actually that wasn't it after all'.

When I met Julian very recently, that was easier, although he's not the sort of person I'd get on with anyway.

How do I feel now that it's over? It merges into history. The only relevant thing about it is next time. There is an awareness of having been given permission to have an affair myself, and that's nice. And if Kate were to have an affair with someone I got on with, I can see it developing into a *ménage à trois*, which I couldn't before. But it would have to be someone who would be willing to take a subsidiary position to me – not in terms of whether Kate preferred him to me, more to do with it being important that I took the lead and he accepted that.

In hindsight, I don't think Kate's affair was threatening to us, for two reasons; firstly because our relationship was not weak to start with, and secondly because I don't believe someone from outside could split us up. Only we can split us up.

When Kate decides to go on holiday, she does not consciously intend to have an affair. Perhaps some part of her knows that the next stage on in her relationship is to have one. She and David certainly discuss the possibility.

What in their relationship makes the eternal triangle possible? They have a stable partnership, though Kate is dependent on David more than either of them is happy with. His emotional centredness allows her to lean, her leaning encourages him to be even more supportive.

The real element that makes an affair possible for them is that they are both committed to the symbolism of it. For David, allowing Kate to have an affair is a way of reassuring himself that he is 'in control'; feeling able to have one himself is also an attraction. Kate seems less clear than David what the meaning of a triangle would be to her, but she is sufficiently undistressed about it to make an affair a real possibility.

From the start of the holiday, we sense that Kate is also clear about her agendas. She keeps well away from men whose agendas may be around a committed relationship, and makes emotional links only with men who are patently not going to threaten her relationship with David.

She gets rejected by one man because of her age, and certainly this does give her an agenda involving proving that she is still attractive. The second man she gets attracted to, largely because they can talk deeply, is much younger even than the man who has rejected her, although this is probably an unconscious agenda for her at the time.

Julian's agendas are remarkably similar to Kate's, and this is one reason why they gel so quickly. He, too, wants a sexual liaison, and Kate is sufficiently attractive – to other men in the group, as well as to him – and sufficiently available, to make her ideal. But also she is safe. She has stated clearly that she is in a committed relationship, and this means that Julian can approach without fearing that she will get too involved. For both of them, the situation is ideal.

From the start, there is no question of secrecy in this triangle. Any thought of it would have been immediately threatening to everyone. All the communication is clear and consistent. So, when Kate gets home, she tells David immediately what has happened. This is, in some ways, the crunch point. Had he been hurt, she most certainly would have withdrawn from Julian and the triangle would not have developed. As it is, he is aroused and supportive, and so Kate feels able to proceed.

The dynamic between her and Julian is a simple one of strong attraction. There is some sexual tension, but it never affects their relationship sufficiently for this to matter. The dynamic is held stable by the fact that neither of them intends to get involved, and we presume that if either of them does move towards that, the other moves back. Whatever, for over three months, the relationship proceeds on a stable basis with regular meetings.

Had David objected, or started to get threatened, perhaps the dynamic would have moved in a different way. However, as it is, his support allows Kate to feel close to him whilst at the same time feeling more and more independent of him. The change that she originally set out to achieve when she went on holiday is happening.

The dynamic reaches its change-point very abruptly. Kate feels happy enough with the situation to invite both men to a party. But the dynamic has only previously worked in a very regulated way; she has spent one night a week with Julian and the rest of the time with David. Her emotions have been neatly compartmentalized. When the two men meet, she finds herself more drawn to David than to Julian and something shifts for her.

While the two were apart, Kate was able to see the symbolism of the affair in the same way as David saw it – as a proof of their maturity. But she has always justified sleeping with Julian in terms of caring for him. Now, when she feels that she cares much more for David, the symbolism of the affair changes. The reality is still just as good, but she sees sleeping with Julian as being in direct opposition to what she feels. She has to stop.

The dynamic flips over, but only the sexual element changes. The new way for all three of them to relate is as friends, and this works. Kate is able to enjoy Julian's company as a friend without feeling she is being pulled in two directions; Julian is able to accept this, as he has always accepted that Kate's primary loyalty is to David; David is also happy with the situation.

What will happen in the future? There seems no reason why they should not go on being friends, though a flip back into sexuality is unlikely. It is possible that David and Kate will still have affairs, possibly taking it in turns so as not to destabilize their relationship too much. As their agendas and the meaning they place on affairs are so similar, they should have little conflict. Only if one or the other of them chooses a partner with whom they get truly emotionally involved will their relationship be disrupted. Otherwise, they may well still be in eternal triangles for many years to come.

12 The eternal square

I met Helen socially; I already knew that she and her partner had split up a few years ago because he began a relationship with someone else, the girlfriend of a friend of his. When I talked to Helen, she offered to contact the others in this eternal 'square', and I eventually talked to all of them.

This set of stories is unusual in that it brings together the viewpoints of four people involved. It is the story of partners Helen and Stuart, of friend Phil coming to stay in their flat, of his bringing his girl-friend Donna with him, of the developing relationship between Donna and Stuart, and of the final break-up of Helen and Stuart's partnership.

Donna, Stuart, Phil and Helen

Donna

For me, it all started when I met Phil on a course in 1986. I wasn't overly attached to him; I think he just happened to come along at the right time for me. We got on well, but it was nothing serious.

When we finished the course, we both took a three-week job in London on the same project. When Phil said that some friends of his, Helen and Stuart, had offered him a place to stay, I was invited too. I actually realised as we were on our way down to London that my relationship with him was over. I remember thinking, 'No, this is not on. I'm going down with him for the job only.' That is significant to me.

I remember meeting Stuart for the first time when we arrived at the flat he shared with Helen; he gave me a cup of tea and I remember him saying, 'Now, I take two sugars, Phil takes two sugars, Helen takes one sugar. You'd better learn it because, if you're staying here, you'll be making tea!' I was too zonked out with driving to notice him really, and I can't say there was any real attraction. By the time we'd moved into the flat properly, Helen had already left for France, so I didn't get to know her before she went.

For the three weeks of the project we actually stayed on a boat that belonged to Stuart. It was clear from the start that my relationship with Phil was wrong. We'd be fine when we were with other people, but as soon as we got indoors I'd need space away from him. He was very over the top about me right from the beginning, and I don't think he'll ever understand that it was never the same for me.

The real thing came along very soon. Stuart started coming down to work on the boat and we saw a lot of him. We got on well, were really friendly, but nothing was obvious at first. Phil didn't notice anything because, in a way, there was nothing to notice.

Something was happening, though; I was getting attracted. It would have been very different if Helen hadn't have been in France, but as it was, Stuart was very much playing the single man. I knew about Helen and the kids, I'd seen them and pictures of them, but it was important to the development of our relationship that she wasn't there.

Things came to a head when we went to the pub one night. I don't normally drink very much, but on that occasion I had about five pints of cider and I ended up feeling a bit queasy. I decided to go out and be sick, and I was standing at the edge of the river bank leaning over, when I lost my balance. Just then, someone grabbed me; it was Stuart. I just collapsed into his arms, and that was when I knew.

After that, we took whatever time together we could. The relationship just developed; we became very good friends, who slept together.

By the end of the summer, when we moved back to the flat, Helen returned from France. She didn't know about our affair, although she could easily have caught us at something if she'd wanted to. I think an outsider would have spotted immediately what was going on. Phil didn't know either. He still thought I was with him. I didn't tell him because I didn't think there was any future in my relationship with Stuart, and I didn't want to push Stuart's relationship with Helen over the edge just because we had slept together.

I didn't feel guilty. I really didn't see myself as splitting them up; in fact, most evenings I'd try to get them to talk to each other and make up. But Stuart couldn't talk to anyone, Helen would talk at him, and nothing was happening. I knew I wanted Stuart, but I wasn't certain it was reciprocal, and I knew that, deep down, he really wanted his kids. So I didn't push things, and I really tried to be a medium to get them back together.

Then Helen got pregnant. It happened one day when I was trying to reconcile them. Helen had come back one evening in a good mood, and had said to me, 'If Stuart doesn't go to the pub tonight, perhaps we can spend some time together, sort it all out.' So when I saw Stuart, I said to him, 'Don't ask any questions, but whatever you do, don't go to the pub tonight.' And he didn't. They disappeared off together, and that was the night Helen conceived. I'm still convinced it was an accident; she didn't mean to get pregnant in order to keep Stuart, because she didn't know about us then. It did make me sure that my relationship with Stuart had no future, that he simply wouldn't leave Helen now.

Then Phil guessed what was happening. I wasn't sharing a room with him any more, though we were both still staying at Helen and Stuart's, and for me the relationship with Phil was completely over. One Sunday, Phil came to the pub where I was working and tackled me about what was going on between Stuart and me, just said straight out, 'I know what's going on.' I had to say, 'Yes, you're right.' I swore him to secrecy, but he said he felt he had to tell Helen. He gave us twenty-four hours to tell her ourselves, and after that he said he would do it.

So Stuart went off to talk to Helen; I just wondered what would happen. I didn't know what Stuart wanted, although by then I was fairly sure that if it came to a choice, he would choose me. I felt sorry for Helen.

That was Sunday. On Monday, Phil came round to see me again; I'd moved out of Stuart and Helen's flat by this time. We got very angry with each other, in fact he beat me up.

On Tuesday, I decided I had to see Stuart. So I went round to the flat. Helen answered the door, and I said, 'Is he here? I'm coming in.' She said, 'No, you're not.' And I said, 'I am,' and burst through the door. Then we all three sat in the living room and talked it over.

In the end, Stuart did choose me, but he decided to spend Christmas and New Year with Helen and the kids, so I went home to my Mum's. I was an absolute wreck all over Christmas, and spent most of the time in tears. Stuart arrived at my place just after midnight on New Year's Eve, and we started living together then.

The next few months were very difficult. Helen wasn't letting Stuart see the kids, and Phil was being really aggressive, threatening our lives, slashing our tyres, smashing up windscreens. Most of it was directed at Stuart, though it was meant for me, I think. Eventually, we ended up on the playing fields, sorting it out, man to man! After that, he calmed down.

Now, life is fine. We have our home, and our baby. We have two of Helen's children living with us and that's great. I have no problems with them; I accept them completely.

I don't feel guilty. My relationship with Phil was over as I was coming down to London and, as far as I was concerned, everything was over between Stuart and Helen when I came along. Up to the break-up, Helen had half a mind to leave herself and make Stuart take care of the kids.

The overlap between Helen and me was only about three months, from my meeting Stuart to his being my partner rather than Helen's. So I really find it very difficult to view the situation as an eternal triangle.

Stuart

It all started when my friend Phil phoned me and asked me out for a drink. He was moving down to London to take a temporary job here, and when I heard he was looking for a place to stay, I said, 'No problem. Come to us.' When Phil arrived, he brought his girlfriend, Donna, with him, and so of course she stayed too.

At the time, things weren't going too well with Helen, the woman I was living with. We were drifting, I was spending a lot of time working away from home.

I was trying to make it work, though, for the kids' sake if for nothing else. At least, I thought I was trying to make it work, but nothing I did seemed to go right. If I got a feeling I shouldn't go to the pub that night, I didn't go. If I was coming home late from work a lot, I tried to come home earlier. It made no difference; nothing I tried to do seemed to work. It was as though our relationship had gone over the hill, was on the downward slope and the brakes weren't working.

I was, if you like, 'open to other possibilities' and had actually taken up one or two already that summer, occasional liaisons with young ladies which had never come to anything. At first, Donna wasn't one of those possibilities. Phil thought he had found Ms Right, so when he told me, 'Hands off. This is really serious,' I believed him and steered clear.

Then, after a while, Phil and Donna moved to stay on a boat we had. Helen was away in France for the summer, with our kids, and I used to travel over to see her, but I also went a lot to work on the boat. Somehow it always seemed to be Donna who came to help me, clad in a T-shirt covered in tar, wobbling around in a pair of wellies, holding a paint scraper in one hand and a blow-lamp in the other! I began to be aware that she wasn't as keen on Phil as he was on her, and that there was something between us. At that point, though, I certainly wasn't looking for an alternative to Helen.

It all happened really quickly. One night we were all down in the pub and Donna, who doesn't drink much normally, had had a few too many. She left the pub and went down to the river's edge to be sick. I thought I'd better go out after her, to see she was all right, and so I did; it's a good job, too, because just as I reached her, she leaned forward right over the river to throw up and lost her balance. I grabbed her just in time, and she collapsed — into my arms.

After that, we slept together whenever we could. It really only took a couple of weeks before I started to see a future for us. The time we spent together was so enjoyable in all respects, and with everything else crumbling around me, I saw her as a way out, a rope dangling to rescue me.

For a long while, though, I followed my usual cowardly course of not wanting to upset anyone. I wasn't prepared to do anything about anything. Helen came back from France at the end of the summer and things carried on as before. The relationship with Helen was going downhill, but we didn't tell her about us; Donna was actually quite keen for Helen and I to patch things up, so there seemed no point in telling Helen what was happening.

In the November, Helen got pregnant. Helen and I tried to get back together, slept together and, for some reason, she conceived. She and Donna reckon it was an accident, but I wonder if it was a con trick. I felt bad about that, and in fact, when the child was eventually born the following summer, Helen didn't let me see her, didn't tell me for ages that she'd been born.

Things between Helen and I broke finally just before
Christmas when Phil found out what was happening between
me and Donna. When he did, it was quite a relief really.
Donna and I sat and talked about it for a while, and then I
decided to go home and face the music.

Strangely, I have no real memory of breaking the news to
Helen. The time is a complete blank. I do remember Helen
coming in at one point the following day and suggesting we
go off to Hampstead Heath. I had no idea what was
happening, but I went along with it, and when we got there
Helen told me that Phil had hit Donna. She'd got me out to
Hampstead Heath in order to keep me away from Phil – and
she was right. I would have done something violent if I had
met him then. I knew by that time that it was Donna I was
going to end up with.

Even then, I was still trying to play the game of not hurting
anyone. I was trying to take the middle road, but I couldn't do
that for ever. In the end, I remember being at home with
Helen and Donna arriving, Helen trying to stop her coming in
and Donna bursting through. The three of us just looked at
one another and then sat down and talked about it. Helen
asked me to choose and, of course, I chose Donna.

When I did that, Helen got up and walked out of the room,
saying, 'I'll leave you to it then.' I thought that was amazing,
and I still admire her for that.

I stayed over Christmas, for the kids' sake, and then left Helen
a few minutes after midnight on New Year's Eve, just taking
with me the clothes I stood up in. I never had any doubts
about whether to leave; I had promised Helen I would stay
until after New Year, and I meant it, but after that I wanted to
be with Donna. We moved in together then, and got married
in the April. The intervening few months were pretty bad,
because Phil was quite violent and Helen kept me away from
the children. We survived, though. That was three years ago.

Now, I have the life I want. I see Helen regularly, and one of our children still stays with her, but the other two wanted to come and live with me, so they do. I still feel a little uncomfortable around Helen. My relationship with Donna is certainly working. I have the partner I want, I have my children round me. It's quite unbelievable.

I know that even if I hadn't met Donna, my relationship with Helen would not have lasted. It might have lasted a little longer, but it was only a matter of time.

Phil

I met Donna on a training course. After the course was over, I went to visit her, and I reckon I was there long enough for the kettle to boil before we went upstairs and made love. The attraction was very strong right away. Her attitude, her joy, her bounce, all really appealed to me. When I went down to London for a project, she agreed to come with me and it was then I started to think of a future together.

I had no idea that she was getting involved with Stuart; things just seemed fine. When it happened, we were all in the pub; Donna went outside for a breath of air, and Stuart followed her. When they came back a while later, nobody looked particularly guilt-ridden, no one said anything at all. I presumed I could trust Donna with Stuart; he had been a friend for a long time.

When we had finished on the boat and moved back to the flat, I suppose I must have picked up on what was happening a bit. There were a couple of times I could have noticed what was happening. Stuart used to get an awful lot of attention from Donna, and often she would listen to him rather than me. But I suppose I thought, 'It's just my imagination,' or 'Well, I don't want to know about it.'

Also, my relationship with Donna was going downhill. She moved out of the room she was sharing with me, and I didn't really understand why. I loved her and I thought I was losing her, so I was very upset. I didn't ever challenge her, though. I don't think I wanted to; I was either afraid I was right or afraid of hurting her if I was wrong.

In the end, Donna told me we had to finish the relationship. I've blocked off a lot of what happened at that time because it was so painful, so I have no clear memories of it.

Eventually, Donna also told me about Stuart. She took time off from work one Sunday lunchtime, and we bought some chips and wandered around eating them. I'm not sure why she told me; I think it may have been because she wanted to start a new life with Stuart and that was one way of breaking the news. It could have been because she wanted to tell me quietly before it all came out into the open. Or it might have been so that I could tell Helen what was happening. I don't know.

At first, I accepted their relationship. I didn't feel to blame, I didn't blame her, I was actually quite happy for her. Then I went back to the flat and saw all the kids' things around and I started thinking. Donna had always warned me that she could not guarantee remaining faithful, but I had trusted Stuart. I felt he had betrayed Helen and betrayed me; I thought he was a right bastard. I wanted to kill him.

In the end, although Donna told me not to tell anyone, I felt the whole thing was so out of order that I had to tell Helen. So I went back to the flat and sat Helen down and told her. 'I'm sorry, but Donna's just said . . .' I think I told Helen that Donna had said not to mention it. Helen was incredibly upset; she had two children and one on the way – and what was she going to do now?

I just got angrier and angrier then. I realized that I'd been lied to for months, and on so many occasions. I realized that when I was out at work and Helen was away, Stuart and Donna had probably been in Helen's bed. I wondered how long I'd been such a mug. The following day, Monday, I went round to see Donna again; she'd moved by this time to a flat nearby. I really lost my temper. I've never been involved in violence, before or since; I run from things like that usually, but I had to let it out that time. We were talking, and then it got to shouting. I really wanted to throw her over the balcony, but instead I hit her. She and her friend just walked off and went to tell the police.

I went back to Stuart and Helen's flat, went into the bathroom and sat on the edge of the bath, crying. When Helen came in and asked what was the matter, I told her I'd just hit Donna – and she took Stuart out for the afternoon, probably to stop him hitting me. In fact, I would have wanted that to happen; most of my anger was against Stuart anyway, because of how he'd treated Helen and the kids.

After that, Donna and Stuart moved in together. They still kept lying to me; they would tell me one thing and then later I'd find out that something different had happened. In the end, though, we did have a showdown. Stuart and I walked out on to the fields and Donna waited in the van. I stood looking at Stuart and said, 'Just walk away, forget it; I won't bother you again.'

I still see them occasionally, but it is still quite uncomfortable being around them.

Helen

One of the things that is really amazing is how little I remember from this time, how much of it I've blocked out. It was one of the worst times of my life, so what I do recall is often in single, unlinked memories.

I know that the relationship between Stuart and I was not very good and hadn't been for some time. When I was with Stuart, I felt he was the one who had the freedom – to go out, work, do what he liked. I was the one who had to stay in. I think I was being very rejecting, due to the fact that I had the kids and felt I couldn't go out and do anything, and he was out spending the money and having a good time. I was very resentful about that, and so cut him off in a lot of ways. In hindsight, I think he was actually trying to be supportive.

The whole thing started during the summer that I went away to France. I'd met Donna before I went, and I remember thinking that she was all right; Phil was totally in love and I like seeing people like that. I took the kids and went to a caravan site for the whole summer, so in a way I left Stuart and Donna the space to get together. Although I had no conscious idea of what was going on. I know that Stuart said he'd come over and see me most weekends; in fact, he came only twice and then was in a desperate rush to get back. I know that at the time I felt very rejected; I thought he didn't want to be with me. The truth was simply that he wanted to be with Donna more because he was having a nicer time with her. I was adding to it, of course, because when he was with me all I was doing was punishing him for not having been with me more.

When I got back, I didn't really spot that anything was going on. It was my Mum who drew my attention to it. She didn't know for sure, but she's very intuitive. I remember that Donna and Stuart took the kids to the cinema to see *Basil the Great Mouse Detective*, and when they got back Mum simply said to me, 'Watch Donna and Stuart together . . . just watch what is happening.' She wouldn't be more explicit than that.

The next thing I remember is getting pregnant. I've thought about whether that was an 'accident' or not, and I really don't know. The first two pregnancies were completely under my control, and so I can't really believe that this wasn't an accident. I don't think I was trying to control Stuart by getting pregnant, but I still wonder why it happened.

Stuart and I made love, and then the next day we went to France together. At the time, I said, 'If I didn't know better, I'd say I had just conceived, though I don't see how that could be possible.' I actually went to the family planning clinic the day after that, and they asked whether there was a possibility I was pregnant; then I remembered the feeling I had had. They gave me some pills to take and they didn't work. To me, that pregnancy was an accident and I didn't mean to do it.

Then, my memory of things gets hazy again. I do remember the Sunday just before Christmas when I found out what was happening. Phil had been to see Donna, and he just came in and said, 'Look, sit down. Donna has just told me that she and Stuart have been sleeping together.'

I was shattered. I felt completely trapped, particularly because I was pregnant. I felt totally rejected, thinking that he didn't love me after all and that the seven years we'd been together had been a total shambles.

We talked and talked. Looking back, Stuart was never anything apart from wonderful. I hated him at the time, but he was very rational, very kind, and would often offer to take the kids so that I could go out. At the same time, though, I know that he was running away from me and going towards Donna. I hated Donna at the time. As soon as I found out what was happening, I told her to get out of the flat. I never wanted to see her again, ever.

On the Monday, Phil came round. As soon as he arrived, he went straight into the bathroom, and I found him sitting on the edge of the bath, crying. I said, 'What have you done?' and he told me he'd hit Donna and given her a black eye. One part of me was really pleased at that because I actually wanted to do it, but the rational part of me got hold of Stuart and said, 'Come on, let's go out for a walk.' I took him off to Hampstead Heath and said, 'The reason I got you to come here is to tell you that Phil's hit Donna.' He went absolutely mad, and it was then I realised just how much he really cared for her.

On the Tuesday, the night of the ultimatum, Donna and Stuart had agreed to meet and he and I had been talking and so he didn't go to her. She knocked on my door, and when I answered it, she just came storming in shouting, 'Where is he?' I screamed, 'How can you barge into my house like that . . .?' The emotion was really high for both of us.

Then we sat down with Stuart and just told him he had to choose. I felt that Donna and I had an understanding that we hated each other, but at that moment I felt we were supporting each other in a common purpose – to find out just what Stuart wanted.

When Stuart had decided that he wanted Donna, in a way it was all right. At least I knew what was happening. I suffered a lot over the next months, but in some ways I didn't want him back. I didn't want him, but I didn't want her to have him. We were cut off from each other completely.

I didn't actually tell Stuart that our baby had been born until a month after the birth. I really felt 'Fuck you, if you don't want the mother hen, you don't get the chicks either!' He's not very strong, so he took the angle that if I didn't want him to see the kids, then he didn't see the kids.

I suppose one of the things that got us speaking to each other again was my wanting him to help with the children. It began by my wanting him to have them a weekend a month, and he agreed to that. Then I said, 'Right – I want you to have them two weekends a month.' When I got that, I said I wanted him to have them a night a week. Then I wanted to go to America for six weeks, and so I said to him, 'Right, you take them. They're your children.' At the moment both the older children live with Stuart and Donna and if our youngest chooses to go and live with them when she's older, then I won't stand in her way.

Now we see each other regularly. I can actually be friends with Donna, which I never would have thought possible. She often phones me up for a chat and talks to me about what looking after kids is like, now that she's got one of her own.

I also realize, in hindsight, that I was actually pushing Stuart away as much as he was wanting to leave. When it all started, I was gathering together my motivation and realising that I didn't actually want him. I really wanted to be on my own.

So, in many ways, I feel that I created the triangle, as much as anyone.

The most fascinating thing about this story is the way in which each person's contribution to the interview combines to make a whole. The whole dynamic, with its agendas, beliefs and lines of communication are all clearly seen not only from one point of view, but from four.

Although it was not clear at the time, in hindsight both Stuart and Helen agree that their relationship was unstable at the start of that summer. Stuart describes it as 'never going right'. Helen sees herself as pushing him away. She knows she does not want him, but, equally, it is vital that no one else has him.

Phil, on the other hand, sees his relationship with Donna as strong and developing. It is unfortunate that Donna disagrees, that the more he moves towards her, the more she moves away.

The two dynamics are waiting to collide.

What are the agendas for each of the people involved? Stuart wants a partnership which will give him fun and happiness, and depth on all levels. He also wants his kids, and fear of losing them is a big issue for him. Donna at first has no conscious agenda around a long-term future with Stuart, and is only conscious of an attraction. Phil wants Donna. Helen probably wants her own freedom more than anything else. It is obvious that Stuart's and Donna's agendas are compatible, given their increasing attraction to each other.

When the spiral between Stuart and Donna tips over into an affair, things start to shift. Helen notices the difference in Stuart, and Phil notices the difference in Donna, although neither of them fully realizes what is happening. The chief shift is that, very quickly, Stuart and Donna realize that the symbolism of their affair is greater than they thought.

Wary of moving too quickly, however, they keep it secret. Donna still hopes that Stuart can develop a better relationship with Helen, because that will give him the access he wants to his kids. Stuart, in his own words, doesn't 'want to upset anyone', and part of him agrees with Donna in wanting to patch things up with Helen. Helen and Phil both unconsciously aid the secrecy, by not challenging what is happening.

As part of this dynamic, Helen becomes pregnant, and we will never be sure whether this is a true Act of God – one of those external events that occur totally outside people's control – or whether she had an unconscious agenda. Helen herself is sure it is an accident, and so is Donna. The pregnancy itself does not keep Helen and Stuart together, for things move much more quickly than that.

The whole situation becomes so unstable that it has to change, and bringing things out into the open is the obvious way to do it. Donna and Phil differ in their recollections of how this happens, but whichever way it does, it has a dramatic effect. It becomes impossible for them all to carry on the way things were.

For Helen and Phil, the news is a terrible blow. For Donna and Stuart, however, revealing their affair is a welcome relief, as it means they can resolve things. It is never really in doubt which way Stuart will turn, for he has been moving towards Donna and away from Helen for a while, though, at first, he needs a push to get him to communicate clearly what his decision is. Donna, initially unsure what he will decide, barges her way into the flat to find Stuart; it is this, combined with Helen's need to know what is happening, that forces Stuart to make his choice – he leaves and sets up home with Donna.

What is the effect on the four of them now the triangle is dissolved?

Stuart and Donna, though still recovering from the trauma, have each other. In time, they build up a solid relationship and start their own family. The triangle itself has lasted for only a few months, and although, at times, its symbolism has been painful, both of them are able to reconcile it in their own minds. They are relieved and grateful they have a future they only previously dreamed about.

It is Phil, who up to now has believed that there is a future with Donna, who erupts into violence, and who, even when Stuart and Donna are settled together, has to work through his anger towards them. For him, the reality of losing Donna is painful, and the significance of being deceived by them both is even worse.

Helen at first finds both the symbolism and the reality of the triangle hard to handle. She suffers a great deal, and reacts by withdrawing the children. However, slowly, as she increasingly gains in self-confidence, she is able to meet her agendas around freedom by meeting Stuart's agenda concerning access to the children. It is only then that she is able to look back and see that although the triangle itself was unpleasant, the results — being free of Stuart and able to live her own life — are actually what she wants. In addition, she is able to see her own part in what has happened and take responsibility for it.

Had any of the elements of the eternal 'square' been different, the dynamic might not have worked out as it did. Had Donna not been with Phil, Helen might have suspected what was going on much earlier, and pulled Stuart back. Had Stuart and Helen's relationship not been rocky, he would not have felt able to have an affair with Donna. Had Helen herself not wanted freedom, she would not have been pushing Stuart away. The eternal square, just as much as the eternal triangle, is created by the sum of its parts.

Action

13 Taking charge

Whether you are in an eternal triangle, entering one, emerging from one, or simply watching a friend go through the trauma of one, you may well be asking what can be done. In a situation that so often seems out of control, the possibility that there might be some way to take charge is overwhelmingly attractive.

The people I spoke to for this book had all, to some extent or another, taken charge of what was happening. They had all been able to resolve their triangle, whether that meant avoiding it, ending it or coming to terms with its continued existence. Some of them were not as successful as others in getting what they wanted; you can influence a dynamic, but you cannot stop the universe. Acts of God do happen and suddenly the whole world collapses around you. Yet from Isobel, who even after her divorce remained in a three-way relationship with her husband and another man, to Stanley, who after twenty-five years is enjoying life alone, they had all survived.

One thing that always impressed me was that, whatever had happened to them, my interviewees had usually come to realize that, as one woman put it, 'things turn out'. However sad they were about what had happened, they had begun to see the possibilities among the regrets. I initially thought that these interviewees were simply experts in post-justification – then I came to realize that most people do make the best of things, and that it is useful to remember this when the worst possible things are happening. Some people were able to realize how good life is without the millstone of a failed partnership, others learned that an abandoned partner was now glad they had left. 'There is always something you can do, however bad it all seems,' said one interviewee, now bringing up his children alone.

So what can you do? The most crucial and far-reaching factor in being able to 'take charge' that I noticed when interviewing men and women for this book was always that of *feeling better about yourself*. It is a cliché of a thousand self-development books, but when seen in action it was, for me, truly startling. This sudden change in self-esteem may have come from a number of sources: going on a course, taking a job, risking beginning a new relationship, having the courage to end one. If, as a result, people felt better about themselves, their situation automatically improved.

In terms of the dynamic in any relationship, this makes total sense. If it ·is the emotions that dictate the direction of the dynamic, then any change in emotions will change the relationship. As the only feelings we have direct control over are our own, and as conscious 'control' of our emotions will not affect the communication anyway, then only genuine, deep-level emotional change will have any effect. The deepest level of emotional change anyone can make is to enhance their own self-esteem — this always works and never fails.

So James's affair with Bindu gave him the confidence to form a long-term partnership with Jeanette; Abigail got herself out of a tricky situation late at night and suddenly realised she could survive alone; Wendy divorced her husband, and started a whole new and rewarding existence.

If you are currently desperate, if you are at present lying awake every night crying, then feeling better may seem an unreal dream — and, in fact, trying to feel better is not what you need to be doing at the moment. Concentrate, instead, on getting the support necessary to allow yourself to cry, to get angry if you need to, to mourn if that is appropriate. Find a friend or go to a professional counsellor. When you have begun to work through those immediate emotions, then will be the time to act.

Then, as you start to recover, begin to work on raising your self-esteem. If you attempt to act while you are still feeling bad about yourself, then you will always sabotage your own actions. When you begin to feel good about yourself through your own courage, through a little help from your friends or maybe through some professional help, then you will be able to take charge.

The first element in taking charge is always to understand the dynamic of the triangle you are in (or are interested in) as fully as you possibly can. Be specific, and do your best to be objective, stepping outside blame and looking at what is really happening in the situation you are involved in. Whichever, use all your knowledge of yourself and other people to ask basic questions, the questions I have been presenting so far in this book about how various dynamics work.

Look first at the **original 'couple' relationship**; it is here that the basic drive towards a triangle begins. Look, too, at the situation of the 'third' person – and their partner if they have one. What is happening in the dynamic to create the possibility of a three-way relationship?

Then look at the factors influencing the dynamic. What **emotions** are being communicated, informing thoughts, words, actions? Who is afraid, who is angry, who is pushing forward, who is drawing back? Are there any patterns to the emotional interaction, particularly ones that have begun to happen recently and may indicate a shift?

What are the **meanings** each person in the triangle places on the affair? What symbolism do they have? What is the effect of an affair on day-to-day life, and how does that make everyone feel?

What are the **agendas**? What does everyone seem to want (or not want) from an eternal triangle; how do various agendas differ from each other; how do they conflict?

What are the lines of **communication**? Where do the really strong emotions, and hence the crucial interactions, lie? Where are the mixed messages, the unconscious communications that may well cause problems?

What about **secrecy**, and how is it used? Who hides what from whom, why – and how does that influence the relationship?

What **movement** is already there in the dynamic, moving everyone away from each other, towards each other, shifting them into new ways of relating, new and more effective configurations? What, if the present trend continues, will the next change-point be; what is the direction in which this particular dynamic is going: towards having an affair, continuing it, ending it?

Next decide what you, personally, want. What are your agendas here and now? Do you want an eternal triangle to begin, to carry on, or to end? Do you want the next change-point to happen, or do you want something different to occur? Remember that agendas can be unconscious and it may only be in hindsight that you realize what you really wanted all along.

Once you have really thought through what you want, the rules are simple.

If the dynamic is moving in the direction you want it to, then keep on doing whatever you are doing. If he is on the point of coming back to you, then find out what you are doing (and particularly, how your feelings underlie your action) to make this happen. Are you encouraging him, withdrawing from him, loving him, supporting him? Do it some more.

If the dynamic is moving in the opposite direction to the one you want it to, then do something different. The plain truth is this. Unless you act, then the dynamic that you are in will continue. If this dynamic is not what you want, then you have to do something different.

This may seem impossible. If you know your lover is about to leave, and you know it is your hanging on to him that is in fact driving him away, how can you stop? This is the Catch-22; there is no answer but to change your emotions.

It may not be your dependency that needs to change. If, by your support, you are enabling your lover to blackmail you into a situation you are not happy with, then the only answer is to stop supporting. If, by your anger, you are driving your spouse away, then you have to give up your anger if you want to keep your spouse. If, by your patience, you are losing your partner, step by agonizing step, then perhaps it is time to lose your temper, very hard and very loud.

We are not talking here either about 'allowing yourself to be trampled on' or about 'being trampled on by others'. We are simply pointing out that if what you are doing is making the problem worse, then there is a simple way to make it better.

You may believe that it is actually up to the other people in the triangle to alter their behaviour, particularly if you feel they have hurt you, acted cruelly, or broken their promises. Unfortunately, you can't make other people change if they don't want to – all you will actually achieve is to make them **pretend** to change because they are afraid of your reaction. The fact is that if you want others to act differently, changing yourself is the best option. Anything you do differently will inevitably affect the dynamic and get a result.

What can you do? These suggestions came from the interviews I held, and are things that my interviewees did to change what was happening for them.

If the **symbolism** you are putting on affairs is working, then you are winning. If you believe that your affair is a celebration of your open-mindedness, and your partner and your lover both contentedly agree, then your triangle is likely to last for years. Conversely, if your affair is the most important thing in your life and this is making your lover back away, can you change what you are feeling? This may seem impossible, but such a change can totally transform what is happening in your dynamic. When Sasha realised that she wasn't dependent on Alex any more, she was able to break free of their unhappy, fifteen-year interaction.

If the day-to-day **reality** of your situation is fine, keep on doing what you are doing. Tamar was quite happy with Alexander's affairs because, 'he was home in time to put the children to bed'. This mattered to her, and the fact that he took that into account helped to keep their relationship stable for many years. If it is the day-to-day issues of any situation that are creating conflict, there are usually very practical steps you can take to alter this. Can you change the things that your spouse or your lover object to, so that everyone has the life they want?

If **agendas** are a problem, how can you get them to match? If you want a one-night stand and your lover wants a life commitment, this probably won't be possible; if, like Kate, you can choose a lover who also wants a fling, and a partner who has agendas about freedom, you may well be able to run a successful eternal triangle for years. If you mysteriously find that what you say you want and what you really go for are different, you are dealing with unconscious agendas, which will always make things messy and confused; try to bring them into consciousness and be clear with yourself about what you really want. Equally, if what you have are mixed agendas, getting clear about how you feel and what you want is the quickest and easiest way to shift your situation to an ultimate conclusion. Be wary. You may find that, once your feelings are resolved, you don't actually want to have an affair/walk out/put up with her infidelity. But at least you will know.

If you are able to bring agendas out into the open, then think about making a negotiated **contract** with your partner and/or lover. Discussing agendas clearly can remove all the unease, giving security and reassurance. However, there are some danger spots. Be careful only to agree to contracts you can live with – if you can't keep up a monogamous contract, don't make one; equally, if you won't be happy with your spouse having affairs, don't pretend you will. If you are afraid that, if you do not agree to the contract your partner or lover is suggesting, then they will leave you, you need to think long and hard about whether you want to be in that sort of relationship.

If secrecy is part of your triangle, then you need to decide whether to maintain it or not. Some interviewees thought that if their partner was turning a blind eye and their lover was happy with secret meetings after work, then they should not break the silence. I am not saying here that lying to a partner is the best way; what I am saying is that this is a choice you have, and one that many people take. Alternatively, one very dramatic way of shifting a dynamic is to come clean. If you tell the truth, or if you allow yourself to 'find out' by challenging your partner, then the backlash will be immediate, but it will change things. If, like Jim, in Wendy's story, you want to resolve your affair, then 'allowing' your wife to read your love letters will do it.

Finally, look closely at what effect **blame** is having on your relationships. There are two classic ways that blame can distort the dynamic. People who feel blamed often, like children, carry on doing exactly what they are being blamed for, to prove that they are acceptable just as they are and that they do not need to give in to other people's disapproval. Equally, other people sometimes keep on blaming rather than simply removing themselves from a situation or making any real attempts to change it. Both are ultimately destructive moves and will perpetuate painful dynamics rather than bringing them to a satisfactory close. However, there is a Catch-22; if you attempt to stop yourself doing either of these, you may well end up blaming yourself for your inadequacy in having blamed in the first place. The vicious circle will simply perpetuate itself. Instead, as I suggested at the start of this chapter, concentrate on building your self-esteem; in the long term, this will always work best.

The interviews that follow all give examples of people who have, in one way or another, taken action. Some have got the outcome they wanted, others have misread the situation and got the opposite response. Some of the ways in which they have taken charge may make sense to you, others may not feel so comfortable. However, all these people have taken action to cope with their situation and all of them have, to some extent, succeeded in their aims.

It is possible. You can act. You can not only understand the eternal triangle, but also take charge of it.

Helen

I had known Stephen since I was twelve and he was rather like an older brother. He developed an infatuation for Jane, a friend of mine the same age as he was. He started taking her out when I was thirteen or fourteen, and then they got engaged. I was quite instrumental in getting them together as a matter of fact and, when it first happened, I was really pleased.

Gradually, I realised that my relationship with him would change, because up to that point Stephen and I had been incredibly close. I suppose I realised I missed his company, the fun we used to have together. As his feelings for Jane grew, so I became less happy with what was happening, though I still didn't really realise what I was feeling. I was only fifteen.

One night both Stephen and I were together in the youth club we both attended, and Jane wasn't there. I was in a very happy and flirtatious mood. I was playing the piano when Stephen came up behind me; at first I thought he was going to tickle me, or get me to chase him, and I felt excited. Then he slipped his hand in my pocket and I could feel that he had put a note there. My heart was pounding because I wondered what it was.

I waited until I got home to read the letter; I was actually trembling because I think I hoped it would be a love letter. Eventually I read it in bed. It said something like, 'I hope you don't mind me writing this. Jane is standing looking over my shoulder as I write it. She has noticed us looking at each other and I've got to emphasize that we've got to be friends, just friends.' The word 'friends' was underlined about four times.

We had all been at a concert together, and Jane thought we had been looking at each other. I don't honestly think I had been looking at him, not in that way. Jane must have been very insecure of him to have acted as she did.

If I had been more sophisticated, I might have recognized the message underneath the expression 'we have to be just friends', the message that he wanted to be *more* than friends. At fifteen, I just took things at face value. I remember feeling very hurt and disappointed because I had anticipated finding a passionate love letter, but I realized that I shouldn't have expected that. After all, he was engaged to someone else. My feelings were very mixed up and confused. I realized, for the first time, that I had much deeper feelings for Stephen than I should have had, considering he was engaged to someone else – think how seriously people take these things at fifteen.

In fact, the letter had the opposite effect to what Jane had hoped.

I think Stephen suddenly felt trapped, that someone had felt they had the right to stand over him and make him write a letter like that. Also, he may not have realized we had been looking at each other when we were at the concert, and her pointing that out may have caused his feelings for me to flare up. He started to feel trapped being engaged to her; he missed the things he'd had with me, the light-heartedness, the understanding. After that he started writing me letters, paying me more attention, focusing more on me and on our friendship.

Then one night, he followed me home from the club, got off his motorbike and said he wanted to talk about the letter. Then he said, 'I can't help looking at you because I *am* in love with you.'

I flung myself into his arms.

Helen's story illustrates beautifully the problems that can arise when acting without thinking what effect your emotions will have. Her original dynamic with Stephen is one based on friendship; when he looks elsewhere to start a more adult relationship, she is able to let him go, although she misses him.

But Jane sees more to their dynamic than certainly Helen is aware of, and she reacts strongly. Her wish, that Stephen write to Helen and 'finish' their relationship, may be understandable, but her emotions turn it into a demand which makes Stephen feel trapped. He does what Jane asks, but her emotions tip the dynamic over; Stephen starts to move towards Helen again and is received with open arms. Jane's demand has been met, but the end result is the direct opposite of what she hoped for.

Kevin

Elaine and I have an open relationship, and it works for us. We've been together for nine years, living together for eight, and from the beginning we've had other lovers.

I've often had more than one lover in the past, and that has always been what's right for me. When I met Elaine, she also had another lover and, although she wanted to have a relationship with me, she didn't want to stop seeing him. We negotiated an open relationship from the very beginning, because both of us like to meet other people and, if you are attracted to others, you like to take it further. I think things would be impossible if we didn't have that kind of relationship.

There is also the issue that Elaine and I can only really have oral sex together; we're both disabled in such a way that we can't move easily from the hips, and full love-making isn't really possible for us. We did try at the beginning, but it didn't really work. We both reckoned that only having oral sex was like getting the hors-d'oeuvre and skipping the main course! Really, although disability is a governing factor, it is by no means the sole reason why we do this; if we were both able-bodied we would both want other partners anyway, probably more so. Let's just say we're both greedy! There are very few things in life that are worth having that are free – and sex is one of them.

I have girlfriends that Elaine knows about, and she has boyfriends that I know about. She goes away for the weekends, and I have a girlfriend to stay while she's away. Often, if I have a girlfriend in for the night and Elaine's around, she'll come in in the morning with a tray laden with bacon, eggs, mushrooms and fried bread! I had to stop her in the end, because it really freaked some of my lovers out!

There are some basic ground rules, though, and I think they are important. First, it is a matter for the individual. If you meet someone and they think they can't cope with an open relationship, you have to respect that or not have a relationship with them. If your partner can't handle it, you stick to that or get out. You can't have your cake and eat it. You can't have it both ways.

Secondly, we insist on condoms because of AIDS and other VDs. I'd prefer to do it bare-backed, but you've got to be sensible. I'd rather lose a bit of the flavour and survive to do it next time.

Thirdly, we are honest with each other. No deception. Elaine is honest about where she's going, and with whom. We've never been tempted to break that rule. There's no point.

Lastly, if one of us wants to have an affair and the other one feels that the partner is wrong, then that's OK. If Elaine says, 'I'd rather you didn't sleep with her,' and her request isn't motivated by jealousy, but by a real feeling that the relationship is wrong for one reason or another, then I say 'fair enough'.

People sometimes don't understand what we're doing. They say that we can't really be in love with each other if we allow each other to have affairs. They say that we're taking a risk that one of us might find someone else and leave.

Certainly there is a danger of that, but there's no point in not doing something just because you're scared. It might happen. You have to take the risk. I don't think love is about being afraid of losing someone; if you need someone you don't love them. Most people form relationships from need rather than want, which means that when their partner takes a lover, they can't handle it – whereas I don't need Elaine, and she doesn't need me.

I actually think some people don't like the fact that we have an open relationship simply because they're jealous. They get very moralistic and judgemental, when in fact they simply can't handle the fact that we are getting it and they aren't!

We do love each other. I think we're stuck with each other now – and that's fine by both of us!

This is a fascinating example of an open relationship that works because everyone is happy with it. Kevin and Elaine are remarkably compatible in their approach. They have identical agendas about the eternal triangle. The significance of it to them is that it makes them feel special; affairs are a sign of maturity and they are proud of that.

The temptation with this interview is to get distracted into thinking that because both Kevin and Elaine are handicapped they can therefore make their own rules. They have no more nor less power to do that than anyone else; to attribute their ability to have an open relationship to their handicap is to miss the point. The real reason they are able to have a working open relationship is that they are both emotionally comfortable with it. Equally, it is not the rules themselves that are important, but the fact that everyone is emotionally satisfied with them.

Julia

It all started in 1986 when I went to work in a garage; Tony was my direct boss.

Almost immediately he asked me out, but initially I refused, largely because he was married. I remember that when he first approached me, one of his friends explained to me that Tony had never done this sort of thing before; he'd been in his marriage seventeen years and had never even attempted to have an affair. He asked me to please take him seriously, so I did. Slowly, gradually, our relationship deepened into an affair.

We really loved each other; it doesn't happen all that often. We never rowed, understood each other so much, wanted the same things out of life.

We went on like this for about three months, a very intense three months, with a lot of emotion going on for both of us. For me, the guilt was very strong, and also the pressure of keeping it all secret. I was so happy that I wanted to share that with everyone, to share him with everyone, and I couldn't – and over it all was this incredible guilt.

Eventually, Tony told his wife, because he's basically a very honest person and couldn't cope with lying to her. She and I didn't meet, but we spoke on the phone, though that just made things worse for her, I think. She really wanted me to be a horrible person and shout at her and call her names so she could hate me, but I wasn't. I was reasonable, in fact I agreed with everything she said – that I was in the wrong.

I thought about things for a long time; I had a constant struggle with myself about what would come out of the situation. I realized that what I would have to do would be to walk away from it and let Tony decide what he and his wife were going to do. If that meant they were going to stay together, then that meant they were going to stay together, and if not, not.

I left. I went down South and got another job.

At first, Tony couldn't understand why I had done it. It took him a long while to realize that rather than running out on him, I was actually doing it for him. I was not saving myself, I was trying to save his marriage by leaving. In the end, he was grateful, because it gave him a chance to pull himself together.

As for his wife, she initially didn't believe he was thinking of leaving. Then it gradually dawned on her what his intentions were. She started trying to keep him by using the children, telling him that the children were saying things about him, that they weren't saying, telling him that, if he left, the children would suffer because they would have to leave their friends. She threw things and created scenes all the time. At this point, Tony realized that staying for the children's sake would be wrong and that it actually wouldn't do any good to stay in the long run.

About nine or ten months after I'd left the North, I got a phone call from him saying, 'I've left my wife. Will you come back?' I must admit that I was scared. I thought, 'Well, it's what I've always wanted and now I have to go and take it'. So I did.

But, for a long while, I couldn't get rid of the feeling that it was my fault. He blamed himself and was angry with himself, though he didn't seem to blame me – but I still felt it was my fault. It was very difficult for me to believe that he could ever feel really happy with me, knowing that I was responsible for the breakup of his family.

We stayed together, but it was hard. I went back to stay with my brother again, and then went back to Tony. We tried living apart. It took so much out of us both that when we calmed down, when things settled down, we began to wonder if being with each other was what we really wanted. Tony was more certain than I was; he said he was prepared to wait for me, as long as it took for me to feel all right about it all. I didn't know when that would be, or if I could do it.

Then, gradually, I stopped feeling guilty. It was a lot to do with going out with my friends more, seeing other people and realizing that what I had done was not particular to me. Other people have gone through the same thing; it isn't just me, and I have to accept what has happened and appreciate what I've got.

So now, we are working through what's happened, coming to terms with it. We've been through a lot, shared emotions, and now we have to make it work.

We will make a go of it. In the end, it is all worth it.

Julia and Tony start an affair which seems right for both of them, but the symbolism of what they have done is totally negative for Julia and she feels guilty.

She moves away, literally but also metaphorically, in an attempt to change things. Things do change. Tony stays with his wife for a while, but then realizes that Julia is important to him. His wife, far from feeling better now that Julia is gone, starts to feel less secure, almost certainly in response to Tony's increasing desire to be with Julia. The situation destabilizes, tips over, and he leaves.

Julia has what she wants. Tony has chosen her and in the short term everything is wonderful. It is her feelings which still stop her from creating the relationship she wants. The situation has changed, but her guilt hasn't; they keep her in a constant spiral of moving away from Tony, who keeps them together by his acceptance of her misgivings. At that point, their relationship seems in doubt – if Julia is not able to resolve what she feels, then they are likely to have continuing problems.

She does, however, take charge. Through interacting with other people, and extending her experience to include other interactions, she begins to feel better about herself and her situation. By doing so, Julia turns the whole situation around, enabling both she and Tony to work on their relationship and 'make a go of it'.

Janet

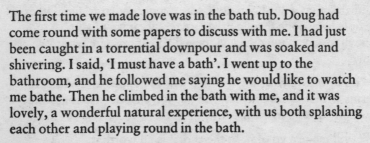

The first time we made love was in the bath tub. Doug had come round with some papers to discuss with me. I had just been caught in a torrential downpour and was soaked and shivering. I said, 'I must have a bath'. I went up to the bathroom, and he followed me saying he would like to watch me bathe. Then he climbed in the bath with me, and it was lovely, a wonderful natural experience, with us both splashing each other and playing round in the bath.

The sexual relationship was good from the start. The more climaxes I have – and I have lots when we make love – the happier he is. Also, he has amazing control and can go on for hours; he just loves to make love.

There are so many good things about it, so many good things to stay in it for. There is a sort of chemistry, a tremendous ease about being with him. I love his amazing enthusiasm. He makes me feel female again, very feminine, yet he actually admires my intelligence and treats me like an equal, never in a condescending way as some men do.

There is the down-side; he is married. He made that very clear from the start, and he is very concerned not to upset the apple cart. He does his damnedest to make sure she doesn't find out. I don't wear perfume or make-up when we're together, for example, and the venue for our meetings changes regularly.

About three or four months after we started seeing each other, I realised that, for me, it wasn't just a fling. I found myself in love, going for long walks and thinking, 'I can't believe this is happening at my age! It must be some sort of mid-life crisis.' This was intermixed with a growing anguish that I would only ever touch, and never really hold on to, this love. I remember one day driving down to the quarry, where nobody goes much, and screaming and screaming until my voice was so raw that I could hardly talk. After all these years, I'd met somebody who was so amazing, and yet there was no way we could have anything together.

I told him how I felt, and it was the only time I've seen him anywhere near anger. Shortly afterwards, he rang and said he felt we should make the whole thing platonic, because it was unfair to me. All along he's been very considerate about this, saying he couldn't give me what I needed and that while I was having an affair with him I wouldn't meet other men.

I was shattered by that. I had to go for a gin-and-tonic – and I don't drink! Because we had a business relationship, we were still able to meet occasionally and that was bizarre. It was like acting in a play, or being in a time warp.

Nonetheless, although I was shattered, I felt that as long as I could carry on seeing him and talking to him, I was happy. And in the end, maybe it was best that the break-up happened, because it got me over the obsessional stage. I came to accept that we wouldn't ever be together, and to take the relationship as it was.

After a while, he started it again. That makes me believe that perhaps he thought that I, or he, or both of us, needed to cool off a bit, and maybe he was right. At any rate, we are still seeing each other and it still works. I'm not as obsessional now; gradually I've come to accept what time we can spend together, and not to expect anything. It's taught me a lot, to live for the moment, and that's taken the pressure off for both of us.

I used to get annoyed, thinking that I was just his 'bit on the side', because he only saw me when it was convenient for him.

I used to get very angry because we always seemed to be slipping in a few hours here and there — we had so little time for ourselves. Then I thought, yes, but you're doing it. It's your responsibility too. Either you accept those terms or you break it off.

I feel very fortunate that I have had this experience at this time of my life. The first forays into the minefield called love are usually pretty dismal. Things improve with experience, and with wisdom, but now I've found the earth really does move. It's not just for the poets.

Janet's relationship with Doug starts happily. When she starts to get involved, however, and it all becomes important to her, she tells him and, in so doing, she triggers him into withdrawing.

For Doug does not want an involvement with Janet; his agenda involves keeping his marriage stable. By withdrawing, however, he triggers Janet into withdrawing too. She 'gets over the obsessional stage' and is able to re-enter the relationship without getting hurt.

The impressive thing about Janet's story is that she does change the way she feels. She does not 'play victim', but accepts that she has chosen to enter the relationship under certain conditions, so therefore she cannot complain of being oppressed. She could have chosen to end the relationship, but instead she genuinely alters her emotional viewpoint so that she can enjoy what Doug has to offer.

Rob

I have to admit I was shattered when I found out that Julie was seeing someone else. It happened like this.

We had been together about a year and things weren't exactly going well between us. It had been very good to start with; we had met almost immediately after I moved down to London, but after a while I think we got into a rut. We would see each other fairly regularly, and stay over once or twice a week, but there was no sense of a future.

In hindsight, I wasn't ready for commitment. I was enjoying being single, enjoying going out and meeting new people, enjoying being in a new town. I had a lot of friends at work, and in some ways being with Julie tied me down.

I think I had noticed that we weren't communicating as well; we had had a few rows, mostly about trivial things. I didn't, however, realize that we were in quite such bad trouble.

I found out in the most clichéd way imaginable – by seeing them together. I walked into a pub in Covent Garden and Julie and Mike were sitting there holding hands. I just stopped dead and then turned and walked round the corner to the other bar and ordered a drink.

I didn't feel able to 'claim her as my own' at all; I was just too shocked. I sat and thought for a while, and then decided to go up and just say hello. I don't think I was going to make a scene, but when I walked round, they'd gone.

Julie and I had arranged to meet the following night, and I spent that day in a state of shock. It was so obvious that she was having another relationship, and that really hurt me. I began to realize she did mean more to me than I thought, although I think I also thought at the time that it might just be a question of sour grapes.

When Julie arrived, I just sat her down and asked her about it. I don't think I was angry, and she says now that I just looked miserable. When I told her I knew, she started crying.

The thing I really had to know was whether the other relationship was important to her. She said she didn't know, that she'd been seeing Mike for about three or four weeks, and that she was very confused. As she put it, 'You didn't seem to want me,' but she said she still loved me.

We spent a pretty bad few days, and in the end did something that I never thought I would do – went to see a professional. We had about six counselling sessions, and the main things that came up were that Julie wanted us to have a long-term commitment to each other, but that I wasn't yet ready for that.

It would be untrue to say that everything suddenly got magically better, but things are different now. I think, for me, the jolt of realizing that I might lose Julie was the main thing, and certainly through the counselling I found out more about how she felt, and vice versa. We haven't rushed into anything, but we are moving in together in about a month, and we'll see how it goes from there.

Julie finished with Mike about two weeks after I saw them. She says that bringing everything out into the open made her realize that it was me she wanted, not him. I think that 'working on the relationship' (as she puts it) made her feel we had a long-term future, and so she was happy to commit herself to me.

Certainly we do now have a future, though I think only time will tell how long that future will be. At the moment we're just taking it a day at a time.

When Rob discovers that Julie has a lover, he reacts very positively, moving towards Julie rather than away from her, giving her a chance to talk things through rather than attacking her.

It is this emotional openness that saves them. Julie's original, if unconscious, need for an affair was linked to Rob's lack of commitment. The fact that Rob is willing to talk about their relationship and eventually go for counselling is direct proof for Julie that their relationship is important to him.

When she has the reassurance she wants, Julie no longer needs her affair. Had she and Rob stayed in their previous uncommitted relationship, it is likely that Julie would have continued seeing Mike – and possibly ultimately transferred her loyalty to him. But her relationship with Rob continues to spiral into increased commitment and so she does not need to. The danger, of course, is that Rob's need for freedom is still there – only time will tell whether they can balance these agendas for life or just for a few months.

Barbara

I've been in every position on the triangle.

The first time was when I was seventeen and I met Joe. He already had a girlfriend, but she had gone to Holland to have a baby, and I was certainly under the impression that she had gone for good.

Then it became obvious that the girlfriend was coming back, and I became more and more aware that I was Joe's 'little bit'. I accepted that because I was enjoying going out with him — but then it became obvious that he was prepared to drop everything, including me, when she needed him. It was a big blow to my ego that someone else could take precedence over me.

The relationship didn't last long, and I got very hurt because I was very keen on him. She got hurt too, I think; one night well after Joe and I had finished, I saw her in a pub, and she came across and poured a pint of beer over my head!

I really hadn't stopped to think how she felt, but I got a chance to find out a few years later when my husband and I got to know a Spanish couple. One evening we visited them and they suggested we stay the night. In the morning, I had to get up to go to a funeral, left John behind and thought no more of it. But then a few weeks later, he went out for the evening and didn't come home.

He rang me the next day at work and asked if he could meet me for lunch. When we got to the restaurant and were sitting down, he just looked at me and said, 'I've got some strange news. I love you.'

I said, 'Yes.'

He said, 'But I love her as well.'

I couldn't handle it. It obviously meant so much to him. In the end, I told him he had to choose between her and me, and then went to my parents while he made up his mind. It took a few days, but then he rang me to say he wanted us to stay together; he asked if I could come back home in about three days.

I agreed, but in fact I came back early and found them together. I was furious; it seemed they had agreed to split up but they wanted to have a few last days together. In the end she left and he never saw her again.

I felt at the time that I must be awful, not sexy enough, that he really wanted her and I was just in the way. My whole self-image went down. Now, I realize that it wasn't me that was wrong. He just met her and was attracted to her. It happens.

After a while, John and I moved to London. There, I got to know Matthew, one of John's friends, and went to stay with him for the weekend. We fell in love, totally. I was completely bowled over by him.

Things were very difficult; John was very jealous and really thought he had lost me. Matthew felt a huge sense of guilt. I felt upset and guilty, although I felt I loved both of them in different ways. When John had been unfaithful and still wanted me, I hadn't understood it at all, but now it was happening to me, I did understand.

In the end, the relationship with Matthew didn't work out; I think he felt suffocated by me, afraid I wanted more from him than he was prepared to give. But he did show me that I didn't want to be married, that my relationship with John wasn't what I wanted. I remember quite clearly thinking, at the end, 'I don't have to have either of them'.

Now, the main thing I've learned is that the worst thing you can do in any situation is to think it's all your fault. You have to accept that, however much you mean to stay faithful, you may meet someone even more wonderful, and so might your partner. Keep a sense of yourself and who you are. Just because your partner leaves you, or you leave your partner, doesn't mean that you are essentially bad.

With experience of all positions in the triangle, Barbara is uniquely placed to understand the emotions from every angle.

It is interesting that what has happened to her is not a lowering of self-esteem as one relationship after another breaks up. She begins by having her ego severely dented, because she is in 'second place', and then doubts whether she is good enough for her husband because he takes a second lover. Then she falls in love herself and, although the experience is painful, she eventually gains confidence and self-esteem from it, and comes to realize that she cannot get her fulfilment only through her relationships. Her ultimate discovery is this: the important thing is to believe in yourself.

Conclusion

As you have read this book, you may well have discovered some surprising things. You may well have had your beliefs challenged at the deepest of levels. You may, as you started to take on a new perspective about affairs, have had to rethink your own attitude to them. If so, perhaps now is the time to stop and take stock.

For myself, I have had my life dramatically altered both by my experience of the eternal triangle and by writing this book about it. I began by thinking of the whole issue as totally beyond my comprehension and control, seeing myself in the centre of a web of relationships which started, developed and ended without my knowing what to do or how to affect what was happening. Through the insight given to me by my interviewees, and through the insight I myself have drawn by creating a cohesive model from what they said, I now see things differently. I can no longer view relationships in general, or eternal triangles in particular, in the same way again.

Perhaps I am being too optimistic if I suggest that this book and its findings will do the same for you. Perhaps it is too much to hope that this book will irrevocably change the way you understand and experience relationships in today's world, or that, having read this book, you will be able always to look for the movements in relationships rather than for the isolated incidents, for the developments rather than for the sudden occurrences, and for the ways in which everyone contributes to what is happening rather than for the ways in which one person is totally in control.

I am an optimist and my hope is that after reading this book you will be unable to see things in the same way ever again. A few weeks or a few months from now, you will find yourself realizing exactly what someone's agenda is in entering a particular relationship. You will find yourself aware of just what the symbolism of a certain partnership is for those involved and how that affects their entire lives. You may find yourself analysing the communication lines in one relationship, or understanding why everyone in another relationship collaborates to keep it a secret. You may find yourself realizing exactly why one triangle works, and why another one doesn't.

You may also discover that you are no longer able to blame. You will, almost without meaning to, find yourself seeing all points of view, realising just what everyone gains from a situation, and what everyone gets. You may still disapprove of a particular relationship, but because of your greater understanding of it, you will find yourself intervening, acting, or changing things, rather than simply whinging about what is happening.

Above all, you will find yourself more in charge of your own life – and this will show itself in the ways you handle triangles that are potential or actual for you. Sometimes, you may use this book to give you the courage to enter a triangle, either to get the love you want or to allow your partner to do the same. You may decide that you will carry on in an eternal triangle, fighting for what you want, changing where you need to change, saying 'yes' and 'no' where those words need to be said. Perhaps you will decide that affairs in any shape or form are not a part of your life; perhaps you will walk away from your lover and his or her partner, or from your partner and his or her lover.

But whether you are entering, maintaining or leaving it, whether it brings you happiness or utter misery, this book will, I hope, give you more choices, more of a chance to understand and act rather than feel helpless and out of control.

For one of the most surprising things I learned as I talked to people who had been through it is that the eternal triangle can be a chance to learn and to grow. As one woman said, 'It was terrible, and I never want to go through it again – but it made me look at myself and other people in a totally different way; I'm more understanding now of what others go through, and I'm more compassionate to myself.' So perhaps, however painful it is for you, you will also be able to use the eternal triangle as a positive experience in your life, transforming it by your under standing into something that strengthens you rather than destroys you.

Even now this book is complete, I am continuing to explore the topic of affairs, and the way that they affect our lives. If this book has helped you to understand your situation or take charge of your life, and you would like to share your experiences, then do write to me. I would be very interested to hear your story.

Susan Quilliam
c/o Pan Books
Cavaye Place
London SW10 9PG

Appendix
Where to find out more

Organizations

If you want counselling on your relationship using the ideas developed in this book, **Transformation Management,** the counselling and consultancy practice to which I belong, can be contacted by writing to us via the publishers:
Pan Books
Cavaye Place
London SW10 9PG

If you want to use family therapy ideas to work on your relationship, the **Institute of Family Therapy** uses similar concepts to work on all kinds of family and couples issues, and can be contacted at:
43 New Cavendish Street
London WIM 7RG

The following are helpful organizations who can support you to explore and improve your relationship, but who do not necessarily follow the ideas and approaches suggested in this book.

Association of Sexual and Marital Therapists
PO Box 62
Sheffield S10 3TS

Brook Advisory Centre
Headquarters: 153a East Street
London SE17 2SD

Catholic Marriage Advisory Council
1 Blythe Mews
Blythe Road
London W14 0NW

Family Planning Association
27–35 Mortimer Street
London W1N 7RJ

Institute of Psychosexual Medicine
11 Chandos Street
London W1M 9DE

Jewish Marriage Guidance Council
23 Ravenshurst Avenue
London NW4

London Institute for the Study of Human Sexuality
Flat C
Langham Mansions
Earls Court Square
London SW5 9UH

Relate (National Marriage Guidance Council)
Herbert Gray College
Little Church Street
Rugby
Warwickshire CV21 3AP

Scottish Marriage Guidance Council
26 Frederick Street
Edinburgh EH2 2JR

SIGMA (Support in Gay Married Association)
BM Sigma
London WC1N 3XX

**SPOD (Association to aid the Sexual
and Personal Relationships of People with a Disability)**
286 Camden Road
London N7 0BJ

Reading

The Eternal Triangle is the first book to deal specifically, and in a popular way, with systemic ideas as applied to eternal triangles. However, there are some more general books that may prove helpful in giving a greater understanding of the overall theory of family therapy.

Families and how to survive them, Robin Skynner and John Cleese, Mandarin Publishing, London, 1983, 0 7493 0254 2
This gives a general and easy-to-read analysis of family therapy as applied to all kinds of social issues.

Foundations of Family Therapy, Lynn Hoffmann, Basic Books, New York, 1981, 0 465 02498 X
This is the definitive textbook on family therapy and its various branches. Quite heavy going at times.

One Flesh: Separate Persons, Robin Skynner, Constable, London, 1976, 0 09 4607120 9
This is Robin Skynner's earlier book on family therapy, written for the lay person.

Thomas A. Harris MD
I'm OK – You're OK £4.99

A practical guide to Transactional Analysis. This phenomenal breakthrough in
psychotherapy has proved a turning point for thousands of Americans.

An important new method of helping people, Transactional Analysis brings a
refreshingly practical approach to the problems we all encounter in day to day
relationships with ourselves and other people. In sensible, non-clinical
language Thomas Harris tells how to gain control of your life and be
responsible for your future – no matter what happened in the past.

Amy and Thomas Harris
Staying OK £4.50

'We need this wonderful book so badly! It is even clearer and more helpful than its predecessor' Harold S. Kushner, author of *When Bad Things Happen to Good People*

Writing with the same sensitivity, insight, humour and compassion that marked their record-breaking practical guide to Transactional Analysis, *I'm OK – You're OK*, Amy and Tom Harris reveal how you can stay that way and get the most out of every day of your life.

Staying OK shows you how you can make crucial changes and take charge of your life. It explains how you can resolve conflicts and root out the causes of worry, panic, confusion, and feelings of inadequacy, depression and regret. The book's message is positive and clear: by maximising good feelings and minimising the bad ones, you can live life to the fullest.

'Their book has a rare commonsense and realism; its examples and anecdotes and snatches of talk and dialogue, whether real or imagined, are representative and convincing . . . if it doesn't work it ought to' THE OBSERVER